THE PATH OF SHADOWS

CHTHONIC GODS, ONEIROMANCY

&

NECROMANCY IN ANCIENT GREECE

GWENDOLYN TAUNTON

MANTICORE PRESS

THE PATH OF SHADOWS

CHTHONIC GODS, ONEIROMANCY, & NECROMANCY IN ANCIENT GREECE

Gwendolyn Taunton

© Manticore Press (Australia, 2018)

Thema Classification: QRSG (Ancient Greek Religion), VXF (Divination), VXWS (Paganism), QRYX (Occult Studies), VXWM (Magic)

978-0-6482996-4-6

MANTICORE PRESS
WWW.MANTICORE.PRESS

CONTENTS

CHTHONIC GODS

DIVINATION & THE OCCULT

CHTHONIC GODS

HADES

HADES

ADJUDICATOR OF THE GODS

THE VAST MAJORITY OF PEOPLE have at least a vague knowledge of the Greek God Hades, due to his portrayal in Hollywood films, which range from Disney adaptations of the myth of Hercules to the Percy Jackson series, and even the ill-conceived remake of the 80's classic *Clash of the Titans*.[1] In all of these cinematic depictions Hades appears as a one-dimensional caricature of villainy, and always in the role of an antagonist or adversary to both heroes and the Gods. Though Hades retains his role as a God of Death and the Underworld, the God's modern media appearances reveal an extraordinarily unsophisticated view of the Greek mythology they intend to display. Hades, despite reigning supreme over the dead, is never classified as an opponent of the Gods within authentic Hellenic Traditions. On the contrary, Hades is the regal

---

[1]   Which is a particularly bad adaption of the original, in the regard that it doesn't have the same storyline, and does not draw on mythological sources, and nor does it even resemble the original film.

brother of Zeus and an ally of the Gods. Hades occupies a role which fills mortals with dread, for as the King of the Underworld, his task is as necessary as it is unpleasant. As such, it is obvious that mortals would revile Hades for separating them from their loved ones and bringing grief to humanity, for death is an inescapable consequence of mortality. However, contemporary depictions of Hades as a villain are not derived from Greek sources but are instead a corruption perpetrated by influences from the Middle East and Christianity.

Although not an antagonist of the Olympians, the visage Hades presents to mankind is nonetheless terrifying, not in a monstrous sense, but rather because he instills in mortals the ultimate fear of the unknown and the deep existential dread of a dark fathomless void without end. Hades is also known as Ais, Aides, or Aidoneus, the original meaning of which is 'invisible', implying that as the final end of life, he lies outside of the sphere of ordinary mortal perception and cannot be seen, until after death or during times when one is close to death. Hades, therefore, is invisible because the living cannot even gaze upon him. Moreover, when the dead enter into his world, they too become imperceptible to humans, save for the *goēs* mentioned in a later chapter who can also perceive the 'invisible' ghosts and shades. The face of Hades cannot be beheld by the living, except by *katabasis* – the perilous descent of the living into the Underworld. The fact that the face of Hades is forever unseen by the living is depicted in iconography. Hades is sometimes shown with his brothers—Zeus and Poseidon—with his head turned back to front, implying that despite his power, he is forever unknown to mortals, in comparison to Poseidon (ocean and earth) and Zeus (sky and aither), which can be experienced by direct perception, as is mentioned here,

> An ancient vase painting shows the three brothers as the three rulers of the world, with the emblems of their power: Zeus with his lightning, Poseidon with the trident, Hades with his head turned back to front. This last was he who might not be looked upon, the dreadful God of death, who caused all things to disappear, who made them invisible. People who sacrificed to the beings of the Underworld had to do so with their gaze averted.[2]

Due to the terrible consequences of looking upon Hades, the Greeks also avoided mentioning Hades directly, and instead referred to Hades through titles, out of fear that saying the name of Hades could attract his attention and inadvertently summon him, leading to a premature demise for the individual who accidentally enunciated his name. Alternative names for Hades which were used to refer to him indirectly included Polydectes (He Who Receives Many) Stygeros (Hateful One), Clymenus (Notorious One), and Pylartes (Warden of the Gate).[3] Hades, despite

[2]   KERÉNYI, C., *The Gods of the Greeks* (UK: Thames & Hudson, 1961), 231

[3]   HARISTA, J., & CHARLES RIVER EDITORS, *Hades: The History, Origins, and Evolution of the Greek God* (USA: 2017)

the horror he instilled in mortals, was still worshiped as a God, with his main cult centers being located at Elis, Pylos Triphyliacus, and at Athens in the grove of the Erinyes.

As the sovereign lord of the third kingdom beneath the earth, and brother to Zeus himself, Hades also has many other names and aspects, aside from his primary function as the ruler of the Underworld. In his more beneficent aspects towards the wholesome dead, Hades is Polydegmon (The Receiver of Many Guests) and Eubouleus or Euboulos (The Good Counselor),[4] both of which imply that he is a gracious host to the deceased he receives into his realms.

Being the ruler of the subterranean world of the dead, Hades also presides over the mineral wealth hidden deep within the earth, such as gold, gemstones, and even more recent treasures such as oil. Due to this, Hades other common name is Plouton (The Wealthy One), from which his Roman name Pluto is derived. This aspect shares some similarities with the Hindu Kubera, who bestows wealth on humans despite being a Yaksha and having a connection with demons in the Vedic era. Like Hades, Kubera is also associated with the pomegranate fruit and treasures hidden in the earth. Kubera is also called Guhyadhipa (Lord of the Hidden) and the meaning of his name is speculated to originate from the root *kumba* (to conceal), which is comparable to the manner in which Hades name stems from the 'invisible'.

---

[4] KERÉNYI, C., *The Gods of the Greeks*, 231

Just as Hades rules the world beneath the ground, his brothers share dominion over the rest of the world, with Poseidon ruling the land and oceans, and Zeus the atmosphere & Olympus. As such, Hades is the exact mirror of Zeus, but not his opponent or 'adversary'. Hades is an equal power and of a similar nature to Zeus, but rules the opposite polarity of the dark earth, just as his brother Zeus rules the bright sky. The power of Zeus is visible, that of Hades is invisible, which is portrayed in both his name and iconography.

Hades, however, is not the original owner of the realm 'Hades', despite the region being named after him. He becomes the custodian of Hades after the conquest of the Titans and their subsequent imprisonment in Tartarus. Though originally a separate region in the Underworld for the incarceration of the Titans, the residency was eventually expanded to include humans who required extraneous punishment, leading to Tartarus also coming under Hades' watchful jurisdiction. The Underworld, therefore, is not Hades' creation; it is bequeathed to Hades after he and his brothers divide power, with Hades reigning as the equivalent of Zeus himself in the Underworld.[5] The close association between the two brothers can be seen in the fact that Hades was sometimes referred to as Zeus Katachthonius or Chthonius, as Kerényi states,

---

[5] HARISTA, J., & CHARLES RIVER EDITORS, *Hades: The History, Origins, and Evolution of the Greek God.*

When mention is made of "another Zeus" or "the hospitable Zeus of the departed", this always refers to Hades. It never means "another God of the daylight heavens", but a ruler of the Underworld who corresponds and is equal to the Zeus of the world above.[6]

Though it has become fashionable in Traditionalist circles to extol the uranic (Sky Gods) at the expense of the telluric/chthonic (Earth & Subterranean Gods), this illustrates an unbalanced perspective of both nature and religion. To value one fundamental requirement of existence at the complete denigration of the other is completely erroneous, and is the major flaw of the Traditionalist school. Life cannot exist without either the earth or the sky, and whilst the uranic impulse may represent creativity, the earth is *reality*, and more often than not, creativity devoid of the pragmatism of reality is naught but a euphemism for folly.[7] The word *khthon* refers to the interior of the earth, from where life is born and returns to after death, which is part of the paradoxical complexity inherent in chthonic cults.[8]

---

[6]   KERÉNYI, C., *The Gods of the Greeks*, 230

[7]   The uranic is falsely identified as male, the telluric/chthonic as female in Traditionalist circles, and anything 'female' is perceived as 'inferior', due to Bachofen's falsified 'research' in mythology which influenced Julius Evola, and in Evola's era, Bachofen had not yet been universally discredited. The fact that Bachofen was a crank, however, is well known today.

[8]   HARISTA, J., & CHARLES RIVER EDITORS, *Hades: The History, Origins, and Evolution of the Greek God*

Zeus is also held to be the father of Dionysus, with the God's mother being either Demeter or Persephone.[9] However, the form of Zeus who begat Dionysus is sometimes referred to as Zeus Katachthonius, a title of Hades. This is why Dionysus is also known by the alternative name Zagreus (The Great Hunter) since no 'prey' ever escapes the traps or snares laid by death, which is an aspect Dionysus inherits from his father. The parentage of Dionysus is also mentioned by Aischylos, who states that he is Hades' son in the Underworld. On Crete, Dionysus was also called Chthonios (The Subterranean) and Zagreus, highlighting his relationship with Hades, not Zeus.[10]

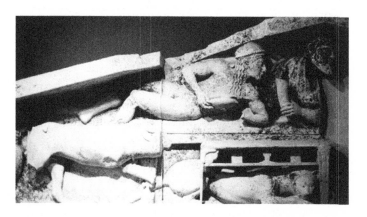

Dionysus with Hades, marble relief, 500 BCE

[9]   KERÉNYI, C., *The Gods of the Greeks*, 252

[10]   KERÉNYI, C., trans. Manheim, R., *Dionysos: Archetypal Image of Indestructible Life* (USA: Princeton University Press, 1996), 83

Although some of his connections with death have been refined in the God's progression from Zagreus to Dionysus, he nonetheless retains his connection to the Underworld, as can be seen in the surnames of Dionysus—as Aigobolos he slew goats, as Melanaisis he wore a black goatskin, and as Anthroporraistes he even slew men—all this in the phase preceding his more benign associations with wine and plants.

Herakleitos of Ephesos expresses the relationship in an even clearer fashion, plainly stating that "Hades is the same as Dionysus, for whom they rave and act like bacchantes."[11] This renders the relation even clearer—Dionysus is not merely the son of Hades— he is an incarnation of Hades that manifests in the world of the living. Kerényi writes that,

> For Herakleitos this identity was a crucial fact, which he could invoke because it was known to all. He used it in support of his own philosophy of the identity of opposites, and because of his philosophy, he was able to recognize and express, as could no one else, the importance of the unity of the God Dionysus and Hades.[12]

Walter Otto also places great emphasis on this statement by Herakleitos and prefers to adhere to this explanation over modern interpretations of Dionysus, as he writes here,

---

[11] KERÉNYI, C., trans. Manheim, R., *Dionysos: Archetypal Image of Indestructible Life*, pp. 239-240

[12] Ibid., 240

This God he says, is the same God as Hades. What can keep us from believing him? Is it his practice to indulge in arbitrary interpretations? His aphorisms, however paradoxically they may sound, bear witness to the nature of things. Should what he saw in Dionysus mean nothing to us? Consider, too, how much he must have known about the Dionysus of the sixth century which is lost to us today. Consequently, his comments must stand as one of the most important bits of evidence that have down to us. We can now understand why the dead were honored at several of the chief festivals of Dionysus.[13]

This is not the only evidence to suggest that Hades and Dionysus are at least related, if not the same God. There is a *calyx* crater which depicts the God Poseidon and his relationship to Dionysus:

In the composition Poseidon looks across to an enthroned God distinguished by a long scepter, situated in the same low region, and to him also point the three serving figures in front of him: an Eros and two nobly dressed Dionysian women standing on either side of a large *krater*, with one woman holding a wine pitcher that is probably empty. The other God is not without resemblance to Poseidon, nor is he lower in rank; evidently

---

[13] OTTO, W. F., *Dionysus: Myth and Cult* (USA: Indiana University Press), 116

> he is the ruler of the Underworld, Hades and
> Dionysus in one, Poseidon's brother.[14]

Otto also links Hades to Dionysus by citing line 330
of Aristophanes' *Frogs* which lists the myrtle as a
favorite plant of Dionysus. Dionysus gave the myrtle
to Hades, at Hades' wish, as a surrogate for Semelē,
which is the basis for the belief that the myrtle
belonged both to Dionysus and to the dead.[15] Similar
connections to the Underworld can also be found in
the symbolism of Ariadne, Dionysus' 'bride'. Ariadne
originally meant the 'holy' and 'pure', and was a
superlative form of Hagne, a surname of the Queen
of the Underworld.[16] Again, this heavily implies that
Dionysus is another form of Hades and that Ariadne
is Persephone.

This association with the dead is also apparent in
the Anthesteria rite, for which there was the popular
expression, "Out of doors, ye *Keres*; it is no longer
Anthesteria",[17] which clearly indicates that 'ghosts'
were banished from the domain of living once the
festival had ended. During this time it was believed
that the dead walked amongst the living, and people
chewed whitethorn and smeared their doors with tar
to protect themselves from the dead. The Romans

[14] KERÉNYI, C., trans. Manheim, R., *Dionysos: Archetypal Image of Indestructible Life*, 297

[15] OTTO, W. F., *Dionysus: Myth and Cult*, 158

[16] KERÉNYI, C., *The Gods of the Greeks*, 269

[17] LANGTON, E., *Essentials of Demonology: A Study of Jewish and Christian Doctrine, its Origin and Development* (USA: Wipf and Stock Publishers, 2014), 81

also had a festival of the dead, Lemuria, held on 9th, 11th, and 13th May, when the *Lemures* and *Larvae*, could enter the house:

> At midnight the worshiper made a sign with his thumb in the middle of his forehead, washed his hands in clean spring water, turned, took black beans and threw them away with averted face, saying nine times: "These I cast, with these I redeem me and mine." The ghosts were thought to gather the beans and follow unseen behind the worshiper, who then touched water, clashed bronze, and asked the ghosts to leave the house.[18]

In addition to this, the Romans had a second commemoration of the dead, which was closer in nature to ancestral rites than the Lemuria. This was the Parentalia or Dies Parentales, lasting from the 13th-21st of February, on which the last day, the Feralia, was reserved for public ceremonies, while the other days were for private celebration by the family.[19]

Hades is, like Zeus, a God of Indo-European origin. Interestingly enough, his history is easier to trace through the hound Cerberus than it is though Hades himself. Cerberus is a well-known mythological figure, who was first named by Hesiod. Hesiod describes Cerberus as the offspring of Typhon and Echidna, and as an "ineffable flesh-

---

[18] TOYNBEE, J. M. C., *Death and Burial in the Roman World* (USA: The John Hopkins University Press, 1996), 64

[19] Ibid.

devourer, the voracious, brazen-voiced, fifty-headed dog of hell."[20] Apollodorus (2.5.12.1.ff), in the second century BCE, is the first to portray Cerberus in the popular form – with three heads, a dragon tail, and his back covered with the heads of serpents.[21] Cerberus, however, is not always depicted with three heads, and the hound also has a dicephalus form, which can be seen accompanied by the figure of Herakles on an archaeological artifact.[22] This is of importance, because the Vedic God of the Dead, Yama, is also depicted with two dogs, as can be seen in the *Rig Veda*: "To thy two four-eyed, road-guarding, man-beholding watch-dogs entrust him, O King Yama, and bestow on him prosperity and health."[23] The other point to observe with the Vedic references is that Yama and his dogs have nowhere near the terrifying imagery of Hades and Cerberus, as was demonstrated in the previous statement, which implies that Yama has the power to also provide health and prosperity as well as bestowing death. The two dogs are also described as benevolent in another passage from the *Rig Veda,* though this instance also makes note of their power to kill.

> The two brown, broad-nosed messengers of Yama, life-robbing, wander among men. May they restore to us to-day the auspicious breath of life, that we may behold the sun.[24]

---

[20]   BLOOMFIELD, M., *Cerberus the Dog of Hades*, USA, 7

[21]   Ibid.

[22]   Ibid., 8

[23]   Ibid., 15

[24]   Ibid., 14

The other predominant character trait of Yama's two dogs is that they are explicitly described as having four eyes, and the two dogs are different colors – one dark, and the other is brindle or spotted.

> Run past straightaway the two four-eyed dogs, the spotted and (the dark), the brood of Saram[=a]; enter in among the propitious fathers who hold high feast with Yama.[25]

In the *Atharva Veda,* one of the dogs is referred to as Śyāma, while the other one as Śabala—meaning brindle—which according to Bloomfield are the correct names for Yama's dogs.[26] This is supported by the Veda of the Katha school (xxxvii) which explains that the meaning of the dog's coloration possesses solar and lunar symbolism, and that "These two dogs of Yama, verily, are day and night".[27] The lunar dog has dark coloration to represent the moon and night, and the brindle or spotted dog represents the sun.

The dogs are referred to as having four eyes because each dog has a pair of eyes, and thus two sets of eyes equal four. Moreover, if they were originally a reference to celestial bodies, it also strongly implies that the dogs are effectively 'all seeing' with their combined gaze. Moreover, the reference to the four-eyed dogs of Yama is clearly related to the Greek

---

[25] BLOOMFIELD, M., *Cerberus the Dog of Hades,* 14

[26] MERH, K. P., *Yama, the Glorious Lord of the Other World* (India: D. K. Printworld Ltd., 2006), 50

[27] BLOOMFIELD, M., *Cerberus the Dog of Hades,* 18

depiction of the two-headed Cerberus, which also has four eyes. The third head was possibly added to complete the Greek planar triad—Uranic (Zeus), Telluric (Poseidon), and Chthonic (Hades)— implying that Cerberus observed all three worlds. Additionally, the *Avesta* also mentions a four-eyed yellow dog which guards the Kinvat bridge,[28] and in another instance Druj (a personification of deceit, falsehood) can be driven away by the gaze of "a yellow dog with four eyes, or a white dog with yellow ears",[29] both of which refer to a solar and lunar dog.

An epithet used to describe Yama's dogs, 'Sārameyaḥ', may also have a connection to the psychopomp Hermes, who guides the souls of the dead to Hades.

> Max Müller observes that the word sārameya approaches very near, linguistically as well as philologically, to Hermeres or Hermes [...] in this functional aspect also Hermes can be compared with the dogs of Yama who have a similar responsibility.[30]

The main difference, however, would be that Hermes is a guide, and the dogs are a guard, though the functions could have, at some point, originally been conflated together. Regardless of whether this

---

[28]   MERH, K. P., *Yama, the Glorious Lord of the Other World*, 55

[29]   LANGTON, E., *Essentials of Demonology: A Study of Jewish and Christian Doctrine, its Origin and Development*, 75

[30]   MERH, K. P., *Yama, the Glorious Lord of the Other World*, 55

inference is correct though, Hermes does clearly have an underworld function which is related to his role as a psychopomp and escort for the dead. Unlike the dogs, Hermes is also officially appointed with this role as a "herald appointed to Hades". Hermes became the messenger and escort to Hades only after a preliminary ceremony had been completed,[31] as can be seen in the following statement attributed to Apollo:

Stele with Hermes taking souls to Hades

And let him alone be herald appointed

To Hades, who, though he be giftless,

Will give him highest gift of honor."[32]

One vital point of distinction between Hades and Yama however, is that Yama's domain is not mentioned as being chthonic in the Vedas. On the contrary, Yama, despite possessing the same functions as a death god, dwells in the Heavens. Out of the three spheres of *dyu* (heavens)

---

[31] KERÉNYI, K., trans. Stein M., *Hermes: Guide of Souls* (Switzerland: Spring Publications, 1976), pp. 42-43

[32] Ibid., 42

which are brightened by the sun God Savitṛ, two are near Savitṛ, while the third-one is a passage for the dead souls to enter the realm of Yama (RV, 1.35.6).[33] Furthermore,

> In the RV, 10.14.8 Yama's abode is mentioned to be in *parame vyoman*, i.e., in the uppermost heaven. It is significant because the third step of Viṣṇu is mentioned to be in the highest heaven (RV. 1. 154.5,6). MacDonell observes that the third step of Viṣṇu is identical with the highest step. The highest step of Viṣṇu is represented as his abode and is also connected with the ideas concerning life after death. The pious men, after their death, live happily in the abode of Viṣṇu (RV, 1.154.5). The RV, 10. 14.8 suggests that parame vyoman is Yama's abode. The VS, 12.63; AV, 6.84.4; ŚB, 7.2.1 TĀ, 6.42 also state that Yama's abode is in the *uttame nāke*, i.e., the highest heaven.[34]

Yama also appears in other religions throughout the Asian region, notably in Tibetan mythology where he is named Yama Gsin-rje as the God of the Dead and also bears the title of the King of the Law (in Tibetan chos-kyi-rgyal-po),[35] which reflects the power of the chthonic Gods to cast final judgment on the actions of mortals. This occurs by appealing to their juridical

---

[33] MERH, K. P., *Yama, the Glorious Lord of the Other World*, 40

[34] Ibid.

[35] Ibid., 270

function, in a later chapter discussing curse tablets. Furthermore, Yama is also connected to Buddhism, which cites Mṛytu as being a messenger of Yama.[36] Boyd, in *Satan and Mara*, also relates the name Mara (the Buddhist equivalent of Satan) to the Sanskrit *mṛtyu* and the Pali *maccu*, meaning death, or to be more specific, *Death Himself*.[37] "Papma", writes Boyd, "is found personified as a God similar to Mṛtyu in Sanskrit texts, but in the literature of the early Buddhist Tradition, there is a complete identification of Papma with Mara".[38] According to Boyd, Papma is never used alone as a reference to an evil personage separate from Mara in the texts. Mara, in later texts, is reduced to being similar to the Judeo-Christian figure of 'Satan', but it is clear that in earlier depictions his characteristics were essentially those of a death God, later vilified as nothing but token opposition for the Buddha. However, when viewed from a historical perspective, the figure of Mara is obviously an amalgamation of earlier Vedic Tradition and emerging Buddhist beliefs. Ling, in his work *Buddhism and the Mythology of Evil*, links Mara to the previous "Brahmanic persona of Papma Mṛtyuh or 'Death the Evil One'",[39] and also to beings such as *Kanha, Yakkhas, Pamattabandhu,*

---

[36] MERH, K. P., *Yama, the Glorious Lord of the Other World,* 48

[37] BOYD, J. W., *Satan and Mara* (Netherlands: E. J. Brill, 1975), 73

[38] Ibid., 74

[39] LING, T., *Buddhism and the Mythology of Evil* (UK: Oneworld, 1997), 56

Raksasas, and *Pisacas.* The use of the word mṛtyuh is a derivative of the Sanskrit term mṛtyu, revealing that Mara is nothing but a version of Yama which has been corrupted by a shift from older Indo-European ideas, to a newer Buddhist framework, wherein the complexity of polytheist traditions based on the natural world have been whittled down to a reductionist perspective of 'good vs. evil'.

This naive reductionism is the inevitable outcome of all monotheism, which inherently lacks a legitimate premise to explain the existence of 'natural evil' in the world, and is thus always watered down to a simplistic view of 'good and bad'. Death, of course, is a natural scapegoat for the philosophical conundrum of evil in monotheism because, albeit an inevitable aspect of life itself, the occurrence of death is almost always unpleasant in some regard. Monotheism has associated death with evil, and it reduced chthonic Gods to the level of scapegoats for 'all-benevolent deities', who cannot be perceived as a source of any woe or ill in the world to their devotees, as otherwise there can be no logical explanation for malevolent and horrific experiences in life. Devoid of an 'opponent' to blame, there would be no war, no disease, no crime, nor any of the unpleasantness which is part of humanities experience and an undeniable aspect of life itself. As a consequence of this, monotheism created an implausible utopia, free from death and pain, which it could not explain, without creating an opposing force from which everything 'bad' arises.

In this regard, Hades, like Yama, has not been spared the inevitable downgrade from a powerful God to becoming a scapegoat for monotheism. However, the portrayal of Hades as an adversary has been the result of woefully inadequate interpretations of Hebrew phrases, and thus the creation of the mythical 'Satan' of Christianity occurs both as a result of mistranslations and the logical necessity of creating a 'strawman' to blame for the existence of natural evil in the world.

The etymological confusion first begins with archaic Hebrew sources. Carus, quoting Budge, states that,

> The Babylonian conception of hell is made known to us by a tablet which relates the descent of Ishtar thither in search of her lovely young husband, Tammuz. It has been stated that the same word for Hades, i.e. Sheol, as that used in the Hebrew scriptures, has been found in Babylonian texts; but this assertion has been made while the means for definitely proving it do not at present exist. The lady of the Babylonian Hades was called Nin-kigal, and the place itself had a river running through it, over which spirits had to cross. There was also 'a pourer of the waters' (which reminds us of the Charon of the Greeks), and it had seven gates.[40]

---

[40] CARUS, P., *The History of the Devil and the Idea of Evil*, (2016), 28

The original term for the Underworld domain of the Christian afterlife, Hell, is derived from the concept of Greek realm of Hades, which does not equate with the modern conception of Hell, but rather with that of Sheol. Christian mythology interprets Hell to be purely a place of punishment, which is not the case with either the Greek Hades nor the Hebrew Sheol. These are the original afterlives for all mortals who had not won the dram of immortality which allowed them to exist in the heavens with the immortals. Thus, Hades and Sheol, are not purely for 'sinners' but the domicile of the ordinary dead. The bleak emptiness of parts of Hades can also be immediately contrasted with the afterlife found in the Elysian Fields and on the Isles of the Blest.[41] Sheol, which has been mistranslated as Hell, simply means the grave or death[42] in its original Hebrew context. In the Old Testament, the word Sheol occurs sixty-four times, out of which it is translated three times Pit, twenty-nine times Grave, and thirty-two times Hell.[43] This illustrates how the meaning of the word shifted from the original interpretation to a Christian description of 'Hell'. There are four words in the original languages of the Bible, which are all translated as Hell, in the common English version

[41] KERÉNYI, C., *The Gods of the Greeks* (UK: Thames & Hudson, 1961), 248

[42] BALFOUR W., *An Inquiry into the Scriptural Import of the Words Sheol, Hades, Tartarus, and Gehenna* (USA: Forgotten Books), 20

[43] Ibid., 9

– Sheol, Hades, Tartarus, and Gehenna.[44] Sheol and Hades simply translate as the grave or an afterlife in the Underworld – only Tartarus and Gehenna are places that correlate with the Christian 'Hell' as a place of punishment. Tartarus is the Greek region of torment in the subterranean realm, originally reserved for the Titans, but later expanded to include mortals who had committed grievous crimes in life, and Gehenna likewise is a place of eternal torment. The name Gehenna "is derived from the Hebrew words *Ge* and *Hinnom*, i.e. the valley of Hinnom […] in this valley, otherwise called Tophet, the idolatrous Israelites caused their children to pass through fire to Moloch."[45] Balfour, quoting Campbell, further elaborates on the origin of the word Hades, and how it came to be associated with the Christian Hell,

As to the word Hades, which occurs in eleven places of the New Testament, and is rendered hell in all, except one, where it is translated grave, it is common in classical authors and frequently used in the translation of the Old Testament. In my judgment, it ought never in Scripture to be rendered hell, at least in the sense wherein that word is universally understood by Christians. In the Old Testament, the corresponding word is Sheol, which signifies the state of the dead in general, without regard to the goodness or badness of the persons, their happiness or

[44] BALFOUR W., *An Inquiry into the Scriptural Import of the Words Sheol, Hades, Tarturus, and Gehenna*, 2

[45] Ibid., 7

misery. [...] This word is also used sometimes in rendering the nearly synonymous words or phrases *bor* and *abre bor*, the pit, and stones of the pit, *tsal moth*, the shades of death, *dumeh*, silence. This state is always represented under those figures which suggest something dreadful, dark and silent, about which the most prying eye, and listening ear, can acquire no information. The term Hades, is well adapted to express this idea.

[...]

It is true, that in translating heathen poets, we retain the old sense of the word Hell, which answers to the Latin *orcus*, or rather *infernus*, as when we speak of the descent of Aeneas, or of Orpheus, into Hell. Now the word infernus, in Latin, comprehends the receptacle of all the dead, and contains both Elysium, the place of the blessed, and Tartarus, the adobe of the miserable. The term *inferi*, comprehends all the inhabitants, good and bad, happy and wretched. The Latin words infernus and inferni bear evident traces of the notion that the repository of the souls of the departed is underground. This appears also to have been the opinion of both Greeks and Hebrews, and indeed of all antiquity.[46]

---

[46] BALFOUR W., *An Inquiry into the Scriptural Import of the Words Sheol, Hades, Tarturus, and Gehenna*, pp. 3-4

Russell also states that the Hebrews had two words for Hell—Sheol, and Gehenna—which the Septuagint translated respectively as Haidēs and Geena. The New Testament makes no clear distinction between Hades and Gehenna, but among the fathers as a whole a vaguely drawn difference emerged: Gehenna is a place of everlasting torment, whereas Hades is a place of purgation.[47] Hades, therefore, came to be known as Hell, and as a consequence of this, was identified with 'Satan' due to a translation error.

This same idea of a purgatory or limbo can also be seen in Roman texts. The Romans often speculated on the geography of the afterlife, with, Virgil (*Aeneid* VI) being the first Roman writer to describe the divisions of 'Limbo', 'Hell', and the Elysian Fields (Heaven).[48] Traditionally, the dead were brought to the realm of Hades by Hermes, where they are met by Charon, who leads them across the River Styx. Charon is based on the Middle Eastern figure Elippu, who is a prototype for Charon in Greek mythology.[49]

When the dead arrive on the opposite bank of the Styx, they are met by the three appointed judges of Hades—Aiakos, Rhadamanthys, and Minos—who decide if the souls warrant being sent to the Elysian Fields, or to be tortured in the dark prison of Tartarus.[50] For those deemed worthy, the souls

47 RUSSELL, J. B., *Satan: The Early Christian Tradition* (New York: Cornell University, 1987), 120

48 TOYNBEE, J. M. C., *Death and Burial in Roman World*, 36

49 CARUS, P., *The History of the Devil and the Idea of Evil*, 31

50 HARISTA, J., & CHARLES RIVER EDITORS, *Hades: The*

are given the water of Lēthē, which blesses them with amnesia so that all the trauma of their former existence is forgotten. Macrobius, furthermore, also connects Lēthē to the God Dionysus, stating that "The astral Crater of Dionysus is a symbol of this mystery; and this is what the ancients called the River of Lēthē."[51] *The Vision of Aridaeus* also links Lēthē to Dionysus, when Thespesius' guide tells him "that this was the way by which Dionysus ascended to the Gods and afterwards too Semelē; it was called the Place of Oblivion (Lēthē)".[52] The most probable explanation for this association is due to the effect of Lēthē on the state of consciousness, much like wine can have, except that drinking from the waters Lēthē brings on a state in which life is forgotten, and consuming the water of Lēthē "separates all states and planes from one another".[53]

With the apparition of the three duly appointed judges of the Underworld, Hades' judiciary function becomes more apparent. Hades does not just reign over the Underworld – like Yama, Hades is the supreme adjudicator of the afterlife, who allots the final fate of souls for all eternity. Moreover, as can be seen with the curse tablets and offerings to Hades, he could also be coerced through magical persuasion to deliver judgment on a living soul, in circumstances

History, Origins, and Evolution of the Greek God

[51] MEAD, G. R. S., *The Vision of Aridaeus: The Most Detailed and Graphic Vision of Hades* (USA), 64

[52] Ibid., 28

[53] Ibid., 65

where the access to human law had been thwarted. Hades, therefore, should be regarded as not only a God of the Dead, but also a God who presides over jurisdiction and the punishment of those who have evaded mortal law by supernatural means. The Erinyes (Furies) could also be unleashed to extract vengeance on a mortal, reflecting the dominion of the Underworld Gods over human legislation – a role which could never be fulfilled by a sentimental deity, which is why Hades presents a cold and aloof demeanor to mortals. Due to his legislative functions, Hades does not form emotional bonds with humans, unlike the other Greek Gods. This legislative aspect also persists in later accounts of Hades. Roman era depictions of Pluto (Hades) in the Sabaziast's *arcosolium* frescoes show a Roman woman being "carried off by Pluto, brought before the tribunal of the Underworld Gods in the presence of three 'Fairies' of destiny (Fata Divina), and lastly led by her 'Good Angel' to a banquet of the blessed chosen by the 'Judgment of the Good', among whom the dead woman is already pictured."[54]

It is Hades' juridical capacity that also explains the nature of punishments in the Greek (and later, Christian) afterlife. The tortures of Hades, originally reserved for the Titans imprisoned in Tartarus, later came to be expanded to include others, notably mortals who perpetrated particularly reprehensible acts, and eventually those who had committed lesser

---

[54] TURCAN, R., *The Gods of Ancient Rome*, (UK: Edinburgh University Press Ltd., 2000), 152

THE PATH OF SHADOWS

crimes, which inevitably led to the Christian concept of 'Hell' being a place of punishment, instead of the dwelling place for *all* the dead. *The Vision of Aridaeus* provides the most detailed description of Hades from classical antiquity, which describes the system of punishment in Hades.

> "There are three kinds of punishment," he continued, "each appropriate to one of the warders and executors [of Adrasteia]. For speedy Punishment (Poinē) deals with those [who] are chastised at once, in the body and through their bodies, but in somewhat mild fashion, since many offenses are passed over as requiring purification only. In the case of those, however, whose moral cure is a more serious business, they are handed over by their conscience (lit. *daimōn*) to Justice (Dīkē) after their decease. And finally, in the case of those who are rejected by Justice as altogether incurable, Fury (Erinyes) the third and most implacable of Adrasteia's ministers, pursues them as they wander and flee, some one way, some another, and pitifully and cruelly undoes them all and thrusts them down into a state of which we can neither escape nor think."[55]

The punishments of Hades, then, can range from minor infringements all the way through to eternal torture. Aside from the Titans, the most severe

[55]   MEAD, G. R. S., *The Vision of Aridaeus: The Most Detailed and Graphic Vision of Hades*, pp. 23-24

GWENDOLYN TAUNTON

punishments bestowed by Hades were issued to the
Danaids, Oknos, Ixion, and Sisyphus. The Danaids
were condemned for murdering their husbands on
the eve of their wedding and forced to constantly
fill a pierced *pithos* with water.[56] Ixion murdered his
father in law Deioneus but Zeus took pity on him and
invited him to Olympus, whereupon the extremely
ungrateful Ixion attempted to seduce Hera. For the
severe affront to Zeus, the punishment is harsh,
with Ixion being strapped to a burning wheel for all
eternity.[57] Sisyphus is also condemned for offending
Zeus, and his punishment is much more well-known
than the previous two incidents, with Sisyphus
having to push a large boulder uphill, only to have to
roll back down to the bottom for all eternity. The case
of Oknos, however, is both the most obscure and the
most interesting. Little is known about Oknos, but
nonetheless, he is referred to as "the procrastinator",
and is condemned to plait a cord from the reeds of
the river of the Underworld, whilst behind him an ass
continually ate the cord away.[58] It is uncertain exactly
what crime the unfortunate Oknos committed, but
Aelian attributes Oknos' punishment to his extreme
indolence. Pausanias, on the other hand, claims that
he had a spendthrift wife, whose way of life obliged
him to work intermittently to cover her expenses but

---

[56] PAINESI, A., Objects of Torture in Hades. A Literary and
Iconographic Study in *Gaia: Revue Interdisciplinaire Surla Grèce
Archaïque*, No. 17 (France: Stendhal University, 2014), 158

[57] Ibid., 166

[58] KERÉNYI, C., *The Gods of the Greeks*, pp. 245-246

to no avail.[59] Given his title of the 'procrastinator', Aelain's explanation sounds more probable, for it would be extremely brutal of Hades to inflict endless torture on a man for the over-spending of his wife. However, Pliny and Pausanias both identify the ass devouring the rope with Oknos' wife—a she-ass—whose exuberant demands apparently continued to haunt him even into Hades, along with an apparent tendency towards procrastination.[60] Whatever the cause of Oknos' immortal plight was, Oknos' fate is definitely the funniest in Hades, proving that Death does indeed have a sense of humor. In Medieval moralized texts, these figures were correlated with Christian sins, with the Danaids symbolizing Gluttony, Ixion as Profligacy and Lust, Sisyphus as Pride, and Oknos as Sloth.[61]

The Vision of Aridaeus also describes lesser punishments bequeathed to mortals, with Thespesius declaring that most piteous of these to behold were the souls of those whose crimes had impacted on their children or descendants.

For whenever one of the latter happened to come up, he fell upon the criminal in a rage, crying out against him and showing him the marks of his sufferings, reproaching him and perusing after

[59] PAINESI, A., Objects of Torture in Hades. A Literary and Iconographic Study in *Gaia: Revue Interdisciplinaire Surla Grèce Archaïque*, No. 17, 163

[60] Ibid., 164

[61] Ibid., pp. 176-177

him. And though he tried to get away and hide himself, he could not; for the chastisers speedily hunted them back to Justice and constrained them all over again, in spite of their pitiful cries for mercy owing to what they already knew of the punishments in store.

And to some of them, he said, many of the souls of their descendants attached themselves, just like bees or bats, crowding thick upon each other, and gibbering in anger at the memory of what they had suffered through them.[62]

With events such as these transpiring in the chthonic realm, it is not difficult to see how Hades developed into being the Christian 'Hell', nor is it difficult to perceive how death would come to be associated with 'evil' in monotheism. In a heavily polarized monotheist narrative such as Christianity, anything even mildly unpleasant would have to be allocated under the broad aegis of 'evil', because monotheism lacks a logical precedent and suitable premise to explain the occurrence of suffering in the natural world. The concept of a being which is all goodness and light, required, as a necessity, the creation of an adversary to blame all the world's problems on, rather than opting for a more cohesive and rational narrative. With death, despite it being a natural occurring neutral phenomenon, it was easy to play

---

[62]   MEAD, G. R. S., *The Vision of Aridaeus: The Most Detailed and Graphic Vision of Hades*, 35

upon irrational fears, and emotive responses, thus rendering the Underworld deities of polytheist traditions an 'easy target' for vilification. Complex Gods were reduced to being stunted, weaker, and morally corrupt opponents who had no authentic goals, save for a monomaniacal tendency to plunge humanity into an irreparable state of ruin.

The transformation of Hades, as a place in the afterlife, occurred before the God Hades was conflated with the mythical 'Satan', and primarily originated with the confusion of the Hebrew *Sheol* with the Greek *Hades*. With the God Hades, however, the transformative process is a different one, which juxtaposes the role of death with that of judging the souls of the dead – and incorporating many different deities from rival polytheistic traditions into the single entity popularly known as 'Satan', which is actually just a word for 'adversary', and, moreover, quite literally, *all* adversaries of Middle Eastern monotheism. As Carus reveals,

> Nothing is more common in history than the change of the deities of hostile nations into demons of evil. In this way, Beelzebub, the Phoenician God, became another name for Satan, and Hinnom (i.e. Gehenna) the place where Moloch had been worshiped, in the valley of Tophet, became the Hebrew name for Hell in place of the word Sheol, the world of the dead underground.[63]

---

[63] CARUS, P., *The History of the Devil and the Idea of Evil*, 46

Gehenna, and not Sheol or Hades, is in fact, the proper name for the Christian Hell, and moreover, it is based on a *physical location* in the Middle East, not Greece. Russell states that,

> These theologians who chose to blur the distinction tended to be universalists, viewing the descent as freeing all the ancients from Hell; those who felt the distinction more sharply believed that Christ descended not to Gehenna, but to Hades and that he saved only the just, leaving sinners in Hell. The distinction—never firm—was further blurred by the translations of both terms by the Latin *inferus*, inferi, infernus, inferni (cf. Fr. *Enfer*, It. *Inferno*, Eng. "infernal") and blurred again in English by the use of the word "hell," derived from the name of a Teutonic Goddess of the underworld.[64] Gehenna is closer to the modern concept of Hell than is Hades, which somewhat resembles the Catholic purgatory."[65]

All of these 'cultural appropriations' and ancient political distortions have led to rival polytheist deities being identified as 'Satan', which makes sense when the title is treated, not as a proper name, but as a title. The original meaning of the Hebrew *Shaitan*, is simply 'opponent' or 'adversary', and indeed, early sources state that there were multiple 'Satans', which over

---

[64] This is another incident of vilification, this time of the Norse Goddess Hel or Hela.

[65] RUSSELL, J. B., *Satan: The Early Christian Tradition* (New York: Cornell University, 1987), 120

hundreds of years, were amalgamated into a single entity, who adopted a role as *the* Adversary. This is a logical requirement for any form of monotheistic belief to explain the occurrence of natural evil, since it cannot possibly arise from the classical theist portrayal of an 'all benevolent, all knowing, and all powerful God'—*it can only arise from an opponent of equal power.* Moreover, in texts which mention Satan as a singular entity, he is not always portrayed as the adversary of Yahweh, but as a high ranking entity who is *subordinate to Yahweh.* He adopts a juridical function similar to that of Hades, accusing humans of sin, and accordingly, overseeing their punishment on behalf of Yahweh himself. In the Book of Zechariah, Satan plays the role of the accuser against humans in the heavenly court.[66] Moreover, Kelly, a Christian scholar, states that, "It is noteworthy that Satan, in the canonical books of the Old Testament, is an adversary of man, but not of God; he is a subject of God and God's faithful servant."[67] Only later in the Christian cycle of myth does Satan 'fall' from God's grace, first by tempting mortals in order to punish them, and finally for judging all mortals to be unworthy and requiring eradication. Thus, Satan, in the New Testament, becomes a powerful adversary who succumbs to his own natural desire to punish Yahweh's imperfect and ultimately unsatisfying creation, humanity.

---

[66]   KELLY, H. A., *Satan in the Bible, God's Minster of Justice* (USA: Cascade Books, 2017), 164

[67]   CARUS, P., *The History of the Devil and the Idea of Evil,* 46

Though Satan and Lucifer are originally different vilified deities,[68] they both fall from Yahweh's grace via the sin of *hubris*, as is seen here in the work of the Egyptian Christian writer Origen of Alexandria – Lucifer rebels against God out of pride.

> 12. Look how the Dawn-bringer (GK *Heōsphoros*, Lat. *Lucifer*) has fallen from heaven, after rising up in the morning! He has been crushed to the earth, he who once dispatched great armies to all the nations![69]

> 13. Once you boasted to yourself, "I will go to the higher heavens, I will establish my throne above the stars of heaven. I will be seated on a great mountain, on the great mountain range of the north!"[70]

> 15. But now you will fall down to the realm of Hades, down to the fundament of the earth.[71]

It is noteworthy that Lucifer, like Satan, is in exile in Hades, and that Hades is mentioned by its correct name, and not as 'Hell'. Origen's conception of Hades was much closer to the original descriptions of the Hellenic Hades as a place of formlessness and

---

THE PATH OF SHADOWS

shadow,[72] rather than the contemporary depiction of a hot, fiery pit, more akin to the lava and the earth's molten core. Rather, Hades is shown to be an incorporeal, fathomless empty void, occupying a chthonic metaphysical level of being, and not a tangible physical plane of existence.

The Christian transmogrification of the God Hades into Satan, the ill-favored servant of Yahweh, is however, never made quite complete, as there are a few instances in which Hades and Satan both feature together, along with Death, thus providing us with an 'Unholy Trinity' in Christianity, composed of Death, Hades, and Satan – all of whom serve a similar function. The *Gospel of Nicodemus* in the "Descent into Hell" narrates the following scene, which verges on being farcical.

> Satan, after having arranged Christ's crucifixion, rushes down to Hell to warn Hades and Death to be on guard against the soul of Jesus as potentially dangerous when he comes to Hell. Hades berates Satan for making a colossal blunder because not long ago this very Jesus snatched away from hell a man named Lazarus, and now he is surely coming to take all the dead away! Suddenly, the gates of Hell are shattered, and Jesus arrives with his angels to rescue the souls of the upright and at the same time to restrain Satan. He orders the angels to tie Satan up, and he instructs Hades to keep him that way until his second coming.[73]

---

[72] RUSSELL, J. B., *Satan: The Early Christian Tradition*, 143

[73] KELLY, H. A., *Satan in the Bible, God's Minster of Justice*

42

It is noteworthy that Hades is depicted as Satan's superior, and highlights the folly of his action, which results in Christ's unwelcome intrusion into Hades realm. Moreover, Christ actually instructs Hades to keep Satan bound on his behalf, suggesting that Hades is not an enemy of Christ, but is still perceived as an ethically neutral immortal. In Revelations, Hades is also mentioned by his proper name, and "Death and Hades are thrown into the lake of fire, along with all people who failed to be registered in the Book of Life" (Rev 20:11-14).[74] In both of these examples, Hades is a separate figure to Death (Thanatos) and Satan is represented as a 'bad employee' of Yahweh, who after having been purged from office, now just exists to tamper with human affairs and thwart the intentions of his former employer.

All of these instances, from the archaic era of Greece to that of Medieval Europe, strongly suggest that Hades was a very powerful chthonic deity, equal to Zeus in his power, who both reigned over the dead and judged them. Hades predates this, however, as Yama the great Indo-European God of the Dead, who shared the three Heavens with Savitṛ as the highest of Gods. Moreover, mortals could also use magical means to persuade Hades to cast a judgment on a living soul or persuade Persephone to unleash the Erinyes. Whilst humans who had been rewarded with immortality could merge their souls with Zeus in the aither or dwell on Olympus, Hades ruled over

(USA: Cascade Books, 2017), 156

[74] KELLY, H. A., *Satan in the Bible, God's Minster of Justice, 156*

the souls of the ordinary dead, as well as serving as the custodian of Tartarus.

As the developing religion of Judaism eventually absorbed all polytheist Gods into its meta-narrative of 'Satans', the meaning of the word Satan not only began to include rival cults, it also juxtaposed the term Gehenna with Hades, through a process of mistranslation, when in fact Hades was closer to the original Hebrew for death and the grave, Sheol. This eventually gave rise to Hades becoming the Christian 'Hell'. It also led to a confusion of Satan with Hades at later points in time. This is partially due to the translation issues, but also out of necessity, for without a scapegoat on which to blame all the pain and suffering in the world there can be no all-loving, all-knowing, all-powerful God to preside over a monotheistic tradition. As we see here, though, neither the Christian devil or Hell ever existed in Judaism, only in its Christian derivative. Rather, Hell is Gehenna, a physical location in the Middle East, and 'Satan' is a composite entity built out vilified Gods from other religions.

One interesting plot twist emerges, however. If Dionysus is the son or an incarnation of Hades, and Hades is associated with 'Satan', then Dionysus literally becomes the figure of the 'Antichrist' that Nietzsche speaks of his philosophy. When Nietzsche asks in his famous statement, "Have I been understood – Dionysus versus the Crucified", the response can only be an affirmative one, but not in the sense that Dionysus is 'evil' in the Christian context. Rather, Dionysus is a God of both Life and Death, a form of Hades reborn in the world of the living. For, as Otto says,

> The madness which is called Dionysus is no sickness, no debility, but a companion of life at its healthiest. It is the tumult which erupts from its innermost recesses when they mature and force their way to the surface. It is the madness inherent in the womb of the mother. This attends all moments of creation, constantly changes ordered existence into chaos, and ushers in primal salvation and primal pain – and in both, the primal wildness of being. For this reason, Dionysus in spite of his association with the spirits of the Underworld, with the Erinyes, Sphinx, and Hades, is a great God, a true God; that is, the unity and totality of an infinity varied world which encompasses everything that lives.[75]

Dionysus, as the son of Persephone and Hades, combines both their characteristics in the concept of rebirth, eternal life, and the hidden solar aspects of the chthonic tradition.

---

[75] OTTO, W. F., *Dionysus: Myth and Cult*, 143

DIONYSUS

THE BLACK SUN
DIONYSUS IN THE PHILOSOPHY OF NIETZSCHE AND GREEK MYTH

"The Birth of Tragedy was my first revaluation of all values: with that I again plant myself in the soil out of which I draw all that I will and can—I, the last disciple of the philosopher Dionysus—I, the teacher of the eternal recurrence…

- Friedrich Nietzsche

IT IS A WELL-KNOWN FACT that most of the early writings of the German philosopher, Friedrich Nietzsche, revolve around a prognosis of duality concerning the two Hellenic deities, Apollo and Dionysus. This dichotomy, which first appears in *The Birth of Tragedy*, is subsequently modified by Nietzsche in his later works so that the characteristics of the God Apollo are reflected and absorbed by his polar opposite, Dionysus. Though this topic has been examined frequently by philosophers, it has not been examined sufficiently in terms of its relation to the Greek myths which pertain to the two Gods in question. Certainly, Nietzsche was no stranger to Classical myth, for prior to composing his philosophical works, Nietzsche was a professor of Classical Philology at the University of Basel. This interest in mythology is also illustrated in his exploration of the use of mythology as a tool by which to shape culture. *The Birth of Tragedy* is based upon Greek myth and literature, and also contains much of the groundwork upon which he would develop his later premises. Setting the tone at the very beginning of *The Birth of Tragedy*, Nietzsche writes:

> We shall have gained much for the science of aesthetics, once we perceive not merely by logical inference, but with the immediate certainty of vision, that the continuous development of art is bound up with the Apollonian and Dionysian duality – just as procreation depends on the duality of the sexes, involving perpetual strife with only periodically intervening reconciliations. The terms Dionysian and Apollonian we borrow from the Greeks, who disclose to the discerning mind the profound mysteries of their view of art, not, to be sure, in concepts, but in the intensely clear figures of their Gods. Through Apollo and Dionysus, the two art deities of the Greeks, we come to recognize that in the Greek world there existed a tremendous opposition…[1]

---

[1] PORTER, J. I., *The Invention of Dionysus: An Essay on the Birth of Tragedy*, (California: Stanford University Press, 2002), 40

Initially, then, Nietzsche's theory concerning Apollo and Dionysus was primarily concerned with aesthetic theory, a theory which he would later expand to a position of predominance at the heart of his philosophy. Since Nietzsche chose the science of aesthetics as the starting point for his ideas, it is also the point at which we shall begin the comparison of his philosophy with the Hellenic Tradition.

The opposition between Apollo and Dionysus is one of the core themes within *The Birth of Tragedy*, but in Nietzsche's later works, Apollo is mentioned only sporadically, if at all, and Apollo appears to have been totally superseded by his rival Dionysus. In *The Birth of Tragedy*, Apollo and Dionysus are clearly defined by Nietzsche, and the spheres of their influence are carefully demarcated. In Nietzsche's later writings, Apollo is conspicuous by the virtue of his absence – Dionysus remains and has ascended to a position of prominence in Nietzsche's philosophy, but Apollo, who was an integral part of the dichotomy featured in *The Birth of Tragedy*, has disappeared, almost without a trace. There is a simple reason for the disappearance of Apollo – he is in fact still present, within the figure of Dionysus. What begins in *The Birth of Tragedy* as a dichotomy, shifts to synthesis in Nietzsche's later works, with the name Dionysus being used to refer to the unified aspect of both Apollo and Dionysus, in what Nietzsche believes to the ultimate manifestation of both deities. In early works the synthesis between Apollo and Dionysus is incomplete—they are still two opposing principles—"Thus in *The Birth of Tragedy*, Apollo, the God of light, beauty, and harmony is in opposition to Dionysian drunkenness and chaos".[2] The fraternal union of Apollo and Dionysus that forms the basis of Nietzsche's view is, according to him, symbolized in art, and specifically in Greek tragedy.[3] Greek tragedy, by its fusion of dialogue and chorus, image and music, exhibits for Nietzsche the union of the Apollonian and Dionysian, a union in which Dionysian passion and dithyrambic madness merge with Apollonian measure and lucidity, and original chaos and pessimism are overcome in a tragic attitude that is affirmative and heroic.[4]

The moment of Dionysian "terror" arrives when [...] a cognitive failure or wandering occurs, when the principle of individuation, which is Apollo's "collapses" [...] and gives way to another perception, to a contradiction of appearances and perhaps even to their defeasibility as such (their "exception"). It occurs "when [one] suddenly loses faith in [...] the cognitive form of phenomena. Just as dreams [...] satisfy profoundly our innermost being, our common [deepest] ground [*der gemeinsame Untergrund*], so too, symmetrically, do "terror" and "blissful" ecstasy...well up from the innermost depths [*Grunde*] of man once the strict controls of the Apollonian principle relax.

[2]   PFEFFER, R., *Nietzsche: Disciple of Dionysus* (USA: Associated University Presses, Inc. 1977), 31

[3]   Ibid.

[4]   Ibid., 51

Then "we steal a glimpse into the nature of the Dionysian".[5]

The Apollonian and the Dionysian are two cognitive states in which art appears as the power of nature in man.[6] Art, for Nietzsche, is fundamentally not an expression of culture, but is what Heidegger calls "*eine Gestaltung des Willens zur Macht*" a manifestation of the will to power. And since the will to power is the essence of being itself, art becomes "*die Gestaltung des Seienden in Ganzen*", a manifestation of being as a whole.[7] This concept of the artist as a creator, and of the aspect of the creative process as the manifestation of the will, is a key component of much of Nietzsche's thought – it is the artist, the creator who diligently scribes the new value tables. Taking this into accord, we must also allow for the possibility that *Thus Spake Zarathustra* opens the doors for a new form of artist, who rather than working with paint or clay, instead provides the Ubermensch, the artist that etches their social vision on the canvas of humanity itself. It is in the character of the Ubermensch that we see the unification of the Dionysian (instinct) and Apollonian (intellect) as the manifestation of the will to power, to which Nietzsche also attributes the following tautological value, "The Will to Truth is the

---

[5]   PORTER, J. I., *The Invention of Dionysus: An Essay on the Birth of Tragedy*, pp. 50-51

[6]   Ibid., 221

[7]   Ibid., pp. 205-206

Will to Power".[8] This statement can be interpreted as meaning that by attributing the will to instinct, truth exists as a naturally occurring phenomenon – it exists independently of the intellect, which permits many different interpretations of the truth in its primordial state. The truth lies primarily in the will, the subconscious, and the original raw instinctual state that Nietzsche identifies with Dionysus. In *The Gay Science* Nietzsche says:

> For the longest time, thinking was considered as only conscious, only now do we discover the truth that the greatest part of our intellectual activity lies in the unconscious [...] theories of Schopenhauer and his teaching of the primacy of the will over the intellect. The unconscious becomes a source of wisdom and knowledge that can reach into the fundamental aspects of human existence, while the intellect is held to be an abstracting and falsifying mechanism that is directed, not toward truth but toward "mastery and possession."[9]

Thus, the will to power originates not in the conscious, but in the subconscious. Returning to the proposed dichotomy betwixt Dionysus and Apollo, in his later works the two creative impulses become increasingly merged, eventually reaching a point in his philosophy wherein *Dionysus* does not refer to a

---

[8]   PFEFFER, R., *Nietzsche: Disciple of Dionysus*, 114

[9]   Ibid., 113

singular God, but rather a syncretism of Apollo and Dionysus in equal quantity, for "The two art drives must unfold their powers in a strict proportion, according to the law of eternal justice."[10] To Nietzsche, the highest goal of tragedy is achieved in the harmony between two radically distinct realms of art, between the principles that govern the Apollonian plastic arts and epic poetry, and those that govern the Dionysian art of music.[11] To be complete and to derive ultimate mastery from the creative process, one must harness both the impulses represented by Apollo and Dionysus—the instinctual urge and potent creative power of Dionysus, coupled with the skill and intellectualism of Apollo's craftsmanship—in sum both the natural creative power of the individual and the skills learnt within a social grouping. This definition will hold true for all creative ventures and is not restricted to the artistic process – 'will' and 'skill' need to act in harmony and concord.

In Nietzsche's philosophy, Apollo and Dionysus are so closely entwined as to render them inseparable. Apollo, as the principle of appearance and of individuation, is that which grants appearance to the Dionysian form, without for Apollo, Dionysus remains bereft of physical appearance.

That [Dionysus] appears at all with such epic precision and clarity is the work of the dream

[10] PORTER, J. I., *The Invention of Dionysus: An Essay on the Birth of Tragedy*, 82

[11] PFEFFER, R., *Nietzsche: Disciple of Dionysus*, 32

interpreter, Apollo [...] His appearances are at best instances of "typical 'ideality,'" epiphanies of the "idea" or "idol", mere masks and after images (*Abbilde*[*er*]). To "appear" Dionysus must take on a form.[12]

In his natural state, Dionysus has no form, it is only by reflux with Apollo, who represents the nature of form, that Dionysus—as the nature of the formless—can appear to us at all. Likewise, Apollo without Dionysus becomes lost in a world of form – the complex levels of abstraction derived from the Dionysian impulse are absent. Neither God can function effectively without the workings of the other. Dionysus appears, after all, only thanks to the Apollonian principle.

This is Nietzsche's rendition of Dionysus, and his reworking of the Hellenic mythos has been forged into a powerful philosophy that has influenced much of the modern era. Yet how close is this new interpretation of the original mythology to that of the ancient Greeks, and how much of this is Nietzsche's own creation? It is well known that Nietzsche (and his contemporary Wagner) saw the merit in reshaping old myths to create new socio-political values. To fully understand Nietzsche's retelling of the Dionysus myth and separate the modern ideas from that of the ancients, we need to examine the Hellenic sources on Dionysus.

---

[12] PORTER, J. I., *The Invention of Dionysus: An Essay on the Birth of Tragedy*, 99

Dionyus on a cheetah,
Pellas, Greece

Myths of Dionysus are often used to depict a stranger or an outsider to the community as a repository for the mysterious and prohibited features of another culture. Unsavory characteristics that the Greeks tend to ascribe to foreigners are attributed to him, and various myths depict his initial rejection by the authority of the polis – yet Dionysus' birth at Thebes, as well as the appearance of his name on Linear B tablets, indicates that this is no stranger, but in fact a native, and that the rejected foreign characteristics ascribed to him are in fact Greek characteristics.[13] Rather than being a representative of foreign culture, what we are in fact observing in the character of Dionysus is the archetype of the outsider; someone who sits outside the boundaries of the cultural norm, or who represents the disruptive element in society which either by their nature creates a change or they are removed by the culture which their presence threatens to alter.

Dionysus represents as Plutarch observed, "the whole wet element" in nature – blood, semen, sap, wine, and all the life-giving juice. He is, in fact,

[13] POZZI, D. C., & WICKERMAN, J. M., *Myth & the Polis*, (USA: Cornell University 1991), 36

a synthesis of both chaos and form, of orgiastic impulses and visionary states – at one with the life of nature and its eternal cycle of birth and death, of destruction and creation.[14] This disruptive element, by being associated with the blood, semen, sap, and wine is an obvious metaphor for the vital fluids themselves, the wet element, being representative of "the blood as the life". This notion of "life" is intricately interwoven into the figure of Dionysus, in the esoteric understanding of his cult, and throughout the philosophy of the Greeks themselves, who had two words for *Vita* (Latin: Life) in very different phonetic forms: *bios* and *zoë*.[15]

> Plotinus called zoë the "time of the soul", during which the soul, in its course of rebirths, moves on from one bios to another [...] the Greeks clung to a not-characterized "life" that underlies every bios and stands in a very different relationship to death than does a "life" that includes death among its characteristics [...] This experience differs from the sum of experiences that constitute the bios, the content of each individual man's written or unwritten biography. The experience of life without characterization – of precisely that life which "resounded" for the Greeks in the word zoë – is, on the other hand, indescribable.[16]

---

[14] PFEFFER, R., *Nietzsche: Disciple of Dionysus*, 126

[15] KERÉNYI, C., *Dionysos Archetypal Image of Indestructible Life* (USA: Princeton University Press, 1996), xxxxi

[16] Ibid., xxxxv

Zoë is Life in its immortal and transcendent aspect, and is thus representative of the pure primordial state. Zoë is the presupposition of the death drive, and death exists only in relation to zoë. It is a product of life in accordance with a dialectic that is a process not of thought, but of life itself, of the zoë in each individual bios.[17]

The other primary association of Dionysus is with the chthonic powers, and we frequently find him taking the form of snakes. According to the myth of his dismemberment by the Titans, a myth which is strongly associated with Delphi, he was born of Persephone, after Hades, taking snake form, had impregnated her.[18] In Euripides' *Bacchae*, Dionysus, being the son of Hades, is a God of dark subterranean forces; yet being also the son of Persephone, he mediates between the chthonic world and earth, once again playing the role of a liminal outsider that passes in transit from one domain to another.[19]

A description of his temple showing his association with nature has been left to us by a physician from Thasos: "A temple in the open air, an open-air *naos* with an altar and a cradle of vine branches; a fine lair, always green; and for the initiates

---

[17]   KERÉNYI, C., *Dionysos Archetypal Image of Indestructible Life*, pp. 204-205

[18]   FONTENROSE, J., *Python: A Study of Delphic Myth and its Origins* (USA: University of California Press, 1980), 378

[19]   POZZI, D. C., & WICKERMAN, J. M., *Myth & the Polis*, 147

a room in which to sing the *evoe*."[20] This stands in direct contrast to Apollo, who was represented by architectural and artificial beauty. Likewise, his music was radically different to that of Apollo's: "A stranger, he should be admitted into the city, for his music is varied, not distant and monotone like the tunes of Apollo's golden lyre". (Euripides *Bacchae* 126-134, 155-156)[21]

Both Gods were concerned with the imagery of life, art, and as we shall see soon, the sun. Moreover, though their forces were essentially opposite, they two Gods were essentially representative of two polarities for the same force, meeting occasionally in perfect balance to reveal an unfolding Hegelian dialectic that was the creative process of life itself and the esoteric nature of the solar path, for just as Dionysus was the chthonic deity, Apollo was a solar deity. They did not represent the physical aspect of the sun as a heavenly body, this role was ascribed to the God Helios instead. Apollo represented the human aspect of the solar path (in this he is equivalent to the Vedic deity Savitṛ) and its application to the mortal realm. Rather than being the light of the sky, Apollo is the light of the mind: intellect and creation. He is as bright as Dionysus is dark. In Dionysus the instinctive natural force of zoë is dominant, associated with the chthonic world below ground because he is immortal, and his power normally unseen. He rules during Apollo's

[20]   DETIENNE, M., trans. GOLDHAMMER, A., *Dionysos At Large* (UK: Harvard University Press, 1989), 46

[21]   POZZI, D. C., & WICKERMAN, J. M., *Myth & the Polis*, 144

absence in Hyperborea because the sun has passed to another land. The reign of the bright sun has passed and the time of the black sun commences – the black sun being the hidden aspect of the solar path, represented by the departure of Apollo in this myth.

Apollo is frequently mentioned in connection to Dionysus in Greek myth. Inscriptions dating from the third century BCE mention that Dionysos Kadmeios reigned alongside Apollo over the assembly of Theban Gods.[22] Likewise, on Rhodes, a holiday called Sminthia was celebrated there in memory of a time mice attacked the vines and were destroyed by Apollo and Dionysus, who shared the epithet Sminthios on the island.[23] They are even cited together in the *Odyssey* (XI 312-25), and also in the story of the death of Koronis, who was shot by Artemis, at Apollo's instigation because she had betrayed the God with a mortal lover.[24] Also, the twin peaks on Parnassos were traditionally known as the "peaks of Apollo and Dionysus."[25] Their association and worship, however, was even more closely entwined at Delphi, for as Leicester Holland has perceived:

---

[22] DETIENNE, M., trans. Goldhammer, A., *Dionysos At Large*, 18

[23] GERSHENSON, D. E., Apollo the Wolf-God in *Journal of Indo-European Studies*, Monograph no. 8 (USA: Institute for the Study of Man, 1991), 32

[24] KERÉNYI, C., *Dionysos Archetypal Image of Indestructible Life*, 103

[25] POZZI, D. C., & WICKERMAN, J. M., *Myth & the Polis*, 139

(1) Dionysus spoke oracles at Delphi before Apollo did; (2) his bones were placed in a basin beside the tripod; (3) the *omphalos* was his tomb. It is well known, moreover, that Dionysus was second only to Apollo in Delphian and Parnassian worship; Plutarch, in fact, assigns to Dionysus an equal share with Apollo in Delphi.[26]

A Pindaric Scholiast also says that Python ruled the prophetic tripod on which Dionysus was the first to speak oracles and then Apollo killed the snake and took over.[27] The association of Apollo and Dionysus in Delphi, moreover, was not limited to their connection to the Delphic Oracle. We also find this relationship echoed in the commemoration of the Great flood which was celebrated each year at a Delphian festival called Aiglē, celebrated two or three days before the full moon of January or February, at the same time as the Athenian Anthesteria festival. The last day of this was devoted to commemorating the victims of the Great Flood, at the same time of the year when Apollo was believed to return from his sojourn among the Hyperboreans. Moreover, Dionysus is said to have perished and returned to life in the flood.[28]

[26]   FONTENROSE, J., *Python: A Study of Delphic Myth and its Origins* (USA: University of California Press, 1980), 375

[27]   Ibid., 376

[28]   GERSHENSON, D. E., Apollo the Wolf-God in *Journal of Indo-European Studies*, Monograph no.8, 61

Relief of Apollo

Apollo's Hyperborean absence is his annual death. Apollonios says that Apollo shed tears when he went to the Hyperborean land, "thence flows the Eridanos, on whose banks the Heliades wail without cease; and extremely low spirits came over the Argonauts as they sailed that river of amber tears."[29] This is the time of Dionysus' reign at Delphi in which he was the center of worship there for the three winter months when Apollo was absent. Plutarch, himself a priest of the Pythian Apollo, Amphictyonic official and a frequent visitor to Delphi, says that for nine months the *paean* was sung in Apollo's honor at sacrifices, but at the beginning of winter the paeans suddenly ceased, then for three months men sang dithyrambs and addressed themselves to Dionysus rather than to Apollo.[30] Chthonian Dionysus manifested when the souls of the dead rose to walk briefly in the upper world again, in the Athenian Anthesteria festival, whose Delphian counterpart was the Theophania.

---

[29] FONTENROSE, J., *Python: A Study of Delphic Myth and its Origins* (USA: University of California Press, 1980), 387

[30] Ibid., 379

The Theophania marked the end of Dionysus' reign and Apollo's return. Dionysus and the ghosts descended once more to Hades realm.[31] In this immortal aspect Dionysus is very far removed from being a God of the dead and winter. Instead he represents immortal life—*the zoë*—which was employed in the Dionysian cult to release psychosomatic energies summoned from the depths that were discharged in a physical cult of life.[32] Dionysus is the depiction of transcendent primordial life, life that persists even during the absence of the sun – for, just as Apollo is the Golden Sun, Dionysus is the Black or Winter Sun, reigning in the world below ground until Apollo departs to another hemisphere, and then reigning in Apollo's absence.

Far from being antagonistic opposites, Apollo and Dionysus were so closely related in Greek myth that according to Deinarchos, Dionysus was killed and buried at Delphi beside the golden Apollo.[33] Likewise, in the Lykourgos tetralogy of Aischylos, the cry "Ivy-Apollo, Bakchios, the soothsayer," is heard when the Thracian bacchantes, the *Bassarai*, attack Orpheus, the worshiper of Apollo and the sun. The cry suggests a higher knowledge of the connection between Apollo and Dionysus, the dark God, whom Orpheus denies in favor of the luminous God. In the Lykymnios of Euripides, the same connection

---

[31]   FONTENROSE, J., *Python: A Study of Delphic Myth and its Origins*, pp. 380-381

[32]   Ibid., 219

[33]   Ibid., 388

is attested by the cry, "Lord, laurel-loving Bakchios, Paean Apollo, player of the Lyre."[34] Similarly, we find another paean by Philodamos addressed to Dionysus from Delphi: "Come hither, Lord Dithyrambos, Backchos...Bromios now in the spring's holy period."[35] The pediments of the temple of Apollo portray Apollo with Leto, Artemis, and the Muses on one side, and on the other Dionysus and the thyiads. A vase painting of c.400 BCE also shows Apollo and Dionysus in Delphi holding their hands to one another.[36]

An analysis of Nietzsche's philosophy concerning the role of Apollo and Dionysus in Hellenic myth thus reveals more than even a direct parallel. Not only did Nietzsche comprehend the nature of the relationship between Apollo and Dionysus, he understood this aspect of their cult on the esoteric level. Their aspects—rather than being antagonistic—are complimentary, with both Gods performing two different aesthetic techniques in the service of the same social function, which reaches its pinnacle of development when both creative processes are elevated in tandem within an individual. Nietzsche understood the symbolism of myth and literature concerning the two Gods, and he actually elaborated upon it, incorporating Schopenhauer's work to create a complex philosophy

---

[34] KERÉNYI, C., *Dionysos Archetypal Image of Indestructible Life*, 233

[35] Ibid., 217

[36] OTTO, W. F., *Dionysus: Myth and Cult*, 203

concerning not only the interplay of aesthetics in the role of the creative process, but also the nature of the will and the psychological process used to create a certain type, which is exemplified in his ideal of the Ubermensch. The Ubermensch derives impetus from the synchronization of the Dionysian and Apollonian drives, hence why in Nietzsche's later works following *The Birth of Tragedy* only the Dionysian impulse is referred to. This term is not just used to signify Dionysus, but rather the balanced integration of the two forces.

The ideal of eternal life (zoë) is also located in Nietzsche's theory of Eternal Recurrence – it *denies* the timeless eternity of a supernatural God, but *affirms* the eternity of the creative and destructive forces in nature and humanity, for like the solar symbolism of Apollo and Dionysus, it is a cyclical event. To Nietzsche, the figure of Dionysus is the supreme affirmation of life, the instinct and the will to power. The will to power is the highest expression of the will to eternal life, and to truth at its apex of exaltation – "It is a Dionysian Yea-Saying to the world as it is, without deduction, exception, and selection… it is the highest attitude that a philosopher can reach; to stand Dionysiacally toward existence: my formula for this is *amor fati*"[37]

Dionysus is, therefore, to both Nietzsche and the Greeks, the highest expression of Life in its primordial and transcendent meaning, the hidden power of the Black Sun, and the subconscious impulse of the will.

---

[37] PFEFFER, R., *Nietzsche: Disciple of Dionysus*, 261

PERSEPHONE

DEATH AND THE
MAIDEN

Blessed is the one of all the people on the earth who has seen these mysteries.

But whoever is not initiated into the rite, whoever has no part in them, that person never shares the same fate when he dies and goes down to the gloom and darkness below.

– Hymn to Demeter.

ONE OF THE MOST WELL known myths that have been passed on to us from the Hellenic Tradition is that of the abduction Persephone. Her story simultaneously conjures images of both breathtaking beauty and bleak tragedy. Serving as an inspiration for a legion of poets and artists, the story of Persephone, the tale of 'Death and the Maiden' remains as vibrant today as it was at the apex of Hellenic civilization. We are all familiar with Persephone's tale, which is as archetypal as much as it is primordial – the epic

71

saga of a beautiful maiden—a *kore*—forcibly taken from a field of fragrant and soporific flowers, and imprisoned in the dark subterranean realm of Hades whilst her mother weeps. Persephone is gone, the flowers wither, the crops perish, and the sun vanishes from the sky. Devoid of Persephone, the earth languishes in perpetual winter. Her mother Demeter, stricken with grief, scours the earth for her beloved daughter, only to discover her enthroned as the bride of Hades, reigning as the queen of the Underworld. It is eventually negotiated that Persephone is to be returned to the earth above, but due to her consumption of food whilst in the Underworld, Persephone was doomed to remain with Hades one-third of the year. This myth is deeply archetypal in terms of symbolism, hence its popularity and persistence into the modern era. To analyze the myth, however, is an onerous task for history has revealed little of the Mystery Traditions which composed the sacred rites of Eleusis, which was the main location for the worship of Demeter and Persephone.

To understand the nature of the unique relationship between Persephone and Hades, it is important to examine the principal actors within the myth itself, and then place them within the context of the archaeological elements unearthed at Eleusis. Therefore, it makes sense to begin with the heroine herself, the maiden Goddess Persephone.

Persephone is what Jung refers to as a Goddess called the 'Primordial Maiden', an archetype that contains all the possibilities associated with

Persephone's fate, from being born to giving birth.[1] She is the daughter of Zeus and the Goddess Demeter, and was abducted by Hades whilst gathering flowers in the Nysaean Fields in the vicinity of the mythological Mount Nyssa. The flowers Persephone gathers are specifically mentioned as possessing a heavy fragrance.

> She was gathering flowers, roses, and crocuses
> and beautiful violets in a soft meadow.
> There were irises and hyacinths and a narcissus
> which Gaia grew as a snare
> for the girl with eyes like buds.
>
> [...]
>
> From its root there grew a hundred blooms
> which had a scent so sweet that all
> the wide heaven above and all the earth
> and all the salt, swelling of the sea
> laughed aloud.
>
> [...]
>
> And the girl too wondered at it,
> she reached out both her hands to take
> the lovely toy, but the earth with wide paths

---

[1] JUNG, C. G., & KERÉNYI, C., *Essays on a Science of Mythology: The Myth of the Divine Child and the Mysteries of Eleusis* (USA: Princeton University Press, 1993), 150

gaped open in the plains of Nysa,
and He Who Receives So Many, the Lord,
sprang upon her with his immortal horses,
the son of Kronos with many names.[2]

It is significant that two other Goddesses were present at the time of her abduction – the Goddesses Athena and Artemis, and in some versions the *Okeaninai* are also present. Both of these Goddesses can also be classified as maidens like Persephone, as they remain unwed. What distinguishes Persephone from the other two Goddesses is her quality of passivity, for Artemis is the great huntresses and Athena is well armed with both war and wisdom. Persephone has no defense against the unsolicited advance of Hades. She is completely powerless, because it is her destiny, as was decided by Zeus, for it is he who bestows permission for Hades to take Persephone as his bride. It is also important that Persephone's cries for help were heard by only two of the Gods:

Only the tender-hearted daughter of Persaios from her cave, Hekate in her shining headband, and the Lord Helios, brilliant son of Hyperion, they heard her crying to her father, Son of Kronos.[3]

[2] CASHWOOD, J., & RICHARDSON, N., *The Homeric Hymns* (UK: Penguin Books, 2003), pp. 5-6

[3] Ibid., 6

Sarcophagus showing Hades abducting Persephone

The significance here is that the two observers are both celestial bodies – the moon Goddess Hecate and the sun God Hyperion. This is suggestive of the fact that Persephone is, like her mother Demeter, an earth Goddess, for the sun and the moon both watch the earth continuously from their vantage point in the heavens. In regard to her associations with other deities, Persephone is also sometimes mentioned as being the mother of Dionysus, another God with chthonic associations. Her fate is an imitation of Dionysian tragedy. As a victim and one who is doomed, Dionysus is the male counterpart of Persephone.[4] The God who is most strongly associated with Persephone, however, is her mother Demeter.

Da was a primitive ancient name for Ga or Gaia; called De-meter or Da-meter and she was named so for her role as an "Earth-Mother".[5] In regard to

---

[4] JUNG, C. G., & KERÉNYI, C., *Essays on a Science of Mythology*, 139

[5] KERÉNYI, C., *Gods of the Greeks* (UK: Thames & Hudson, 1961), 184

her relationship with Zeus, Demeter is very similar to Zeus' own mother, the Goddess Rhea, and it is from her union with the God Zeus that Persephone is born. She was also known as Anesidora, Chloe ("the Green One"), Karpophoros ("Bringer of Fruit") and Horephoros (bringer of the favorable season).[6] In her relationship with plant life, it is a matter of perspective as to whether she was the Goddess of vegetation, or was the fertile earth beneath it which provided the necessary nutrients for plant life to flourish.

Zeus was not Demeter's only partner, she also bore children to his brother Poseidon. This illustrates the *hieros gamos* of earth to both the sky and sea successively. Through her relationship with Poseidon Demeter gives birth to the famous steed Arion, the black-maned horse,[7] and a daughter who was called 'Mistress' or simply 'She Who is Not to be Named'. Pausanias mentions this second daughter, whom he calls 'Despoina', but he does not reveal her true name.[8]

Demeter was a popular deity who had very strong connections to the rites of Eleusis. This association of Demeter with Eleusis originates in the Homeric Hymn to Demeter when Demeter reveals her true identity to Queen Metaneira and the inhabitants of the city of Eleusis. She instructs the Eleusinians to

---

[6] JUNG, C. G., & KERÉNYI, C., *Essays on a Science of Mythology*, 114

[7] KERÉNYI, C., *Gods of the Greeks*, 185

[8] JUNG, C. G., & KERÉNYI, C., *Essays on a Science of Mythology*, 180

propitiate her anger by building her "a temple and an altar below it".[9] Saying,

> But come, let all the people build for me a great temple and an altar beneath it, below the steep walls of the city above Kallichoron, upon the rising hill.[10]

Though Eleusis is the site most often associated with Demeter, her annual celebration was spread out over eight days and occurred in different locales. The festival relocated from Eleusis to the heart of Athens, then to the Telesterion, and then returned to the center in Athens. The Eleusinian Mysteries were an annual festival to Demeter held during the middle month of Boedromion, which corresponds to late September/early October.[11] The preliminary rites which were associated with the Greater Mysteries of Demeter occurred in Athens before the pilgrimage back to Eleusis, starting on the 14th day of the month of Boedromion with the transfer of the *heira* (sacred objects) from the sanctuary in Eleusis to the Eleusinian sanctuary on the edge of the Athenian *agora*.[12] The festival began in Athens on Boedromion 16th, on the 17th the celebrants were summoned to the

---

[9] EVANS, N. A., Sanctuaries, Sacrifices, and the Eleusinian Mysteries in *Numen*, Vol.49 (Netherlands: Brill, 2002), 227

[10] CASHFORD, J., & RICHARDSON, N., *The Homeric Hymns*, 16

[11] EVANS, N. A., Sanctuaries, Sacrifices, and the Eleusinian Mysteries in *Numen*, Vol.49, 230

[12] Ibid., 239

sea, and on the 19th the procession began, in order to reach Eleusis by nightfall.[13]

> The 19th of Boedrominian was the time of the great journey from Athens to Eleusis, a 14 mile pilgrimage during which the priests, priestess, magistrates and the *ephebes* accompanied the heira and led the *mystai* along the sacred way. [...] on the night of the 20th the mystai passed through the gates and interior courtyards, and entered the Telesterion where the *teletai* took place, the holy *mysteria* we still know so little about.[14]

Eleusis was located on the southeast slope of a hill overlooking the bay of Salamis and the earliest verifiable sanctuary at the site is a small eighth-century temple built on a man-made terrace and surrounded by a *peribolos* wall.[15] In each subsequent enlargement of the temple that occurred, the Telesterion became increasingly larger, which over time began to assume the appearance of an indoor, square theater.[16]

> The Telesterion was called Demeter's temple, *neos*, and was like all Greek Temples located within a sacred precinct, or *temenos*, separate

[13] JUNG, C. G., *&* KERÉNYI, C., *Essays on a Science of Mythology*, 139

[14] EVANS, N. A., Sanctuaries, Sacrifices, and the Eleusinian Mysteries in *Numen*, Vol.49, 240

[15] Ibid., 233

[16] Ibid., 234

from the inhabited territory outside it. Only worshipers of Demeter's mysteries, called initiates or mystai, were allowed beyond the gates that led into the Goddess' sacred precinct which included the Telesterion and the paved courtyard around it. Outside the sanctuary was a public courtyard containing less sacred sites: a Roman period temple to Artemis Propylaia (Artemis of the Portals), several older altars, including ground altars or *escharai*, and the Kallichoron Well, known from the Homeric Hymn to Demeter to be associated with the myth of Demeter's wanderings to Eleusis after Hades abducted her daughter.[17]

The central temple that defined the Roman era sanctuary appears to have been dedicated to Persephone, however, not Demeter.[18] An inscription found in the Isthmia region mentions the construction of a Plutoneion (a sanctuary of the Roman Underworld God Pluto). Sites dedicated to Pluto are rare, and it is highly likely that the presence of one at this location is indicative of a connection here.[19]

Demeter was also worshiped in Corinth. Archaeological remains from the sanctuaries

---

[17]   EVANS, N. A., Sanctuaries, Sacrifices, and the Eleusinian Mysteries in *Numen*, Vol.49, 236

[18]   DE MARIS, R. E., Demeter in Roman Corinth: Local Development in a Mediterranean Religion in *Numen*, Vol. 42 (Netherlands: Brill, 1995), 108

[19]   Ibid., 109

on Acrocorinth, and elsewhere in Corinthia, demonstrate that Demeter's cult survived the Roman sacking of Corinth in 146 BCE. After this, however, the general direction of Demeter's worship changed. Her chthonic aspect became dominant in the Roman period, and the earlier Greek emphasis on the fertility of the earth was supplanted by emerging funerary and Underworld traits.[20] Thus, the archaeological record points to a change in Demeter's worship, not in terms of a waxing and waning in popularity, but a shift in the orientation of her symbolism.[21] Demeter's connection to the Underworld in this location is, furthermore, only an enhancement of a pre-existing characteristic. Her association with the Underworld has always been present, but it is only after the Roman incursion that her deathly and chthonic aspects are summoned to the fore. A full examination of the Corinthian sanctuary curse tablets has yet to appear in print because their poor condition has made them difficult to decipher, but it is well known that they were addressed to Demeter's chthonic aspect.[22]

It is unsurprising that a Goddess linked to crops & horticulture has an association with death. Following the end of the harvest, the earth no longer rears fruit or vegetables – to all appearances the earth is dead. Life retreats underground where the roots and seeds lie dormant in the soil. It is, therefore, natural that the

---

[20] DE MARIS, R. E., Demeter in Roman Corinth: Local Development in a Mediterranean Religion in *Numen*, Vol. 42, 105

[21] Ibid., 107

[22] Ibid., 108

Goddess of the harvest should also be associated with the shadowy realm beneath the ground. The esoteric revelation of this process is the very essence of the mysteries of Eleusis. The mythical king of Eleusis and his sons, all learn Demeter's secrets, which even the poets cannot disclose.[23]

There is scant information surrounding the rites of Eleusis, though it is known that the *Mysteria* consisted of three parts, *dromena, deiknumena, legomena* ("things done", "things shown," and "things spoken"), none of which necessarily signify ritual practices, though some have speculated that these phrases relate to dramatic performances. From the description of the terms, that occurs is actually a psychological process tied to concept of destiny, since it is easy to draw a parallel betwixt the three terms

and the Fates (Morai). This would explain the trinity of Persephone, Demeter, and Hekate within the ritual space – the combination of the three Goddesses with an earlier Greek Tradition (bearing in mind that the lineage of Tradition which

Demeter and Persephone, marble relief, 500-475 BCE, Eleusis

---

[23] JUNG, C. G., & KERÉNYI, C., *Essays on a Science of Mythology*, 114

identifies the Morai as being extremely archaic, and probably predating Zeus) into a juxtaposition of the two trinities is plausible.

A famous Aristotle fragment comments about initiates to the mysteries: he reports that initiates become worthy not so much because they learn something new (mathein) but because they suffer or experience (pathein) something appropriate to the proceedings.[24] The acts of 'doing', 'saying', and 'showing' indicates that the rites were not a stage play. The archaeological findings are decisively against the supposition of a mystery-theatre, either in the Telesterion or outside it.[25] Moreover, the word for betraying the mysteries meant "to reveal by indirect gestures".[26] This implies that the rites had some form of physical signals associated with them, but the meaning of the phrase cannot be confirmed. However, the formula for the initiate's confession has been preserved.

> I have fasted; I have drunk the mixed drink; I have taken out of the *cista* [little chest], worked with it, and then laid it in the basket and out of the basket into the cista.[27]

---

[24] EVANS, N. A., Sanctuaries, Sacrifices, and the Eleusinian Mysteries in *Numen*, Vol.49, 249

[25] JUNG, C. G., & KERÉNYI, C., *Essays on a Science of Mythology*, 141

[26] Ibid., 135

[27] Ibid., 138

It is also known that unique vessels called *kernoi* and *plemochoai* were used for depositing offers of grains and other plant sacrifices. The Homeric Hymn to Demeter also testifies to the consumption of the sacred drink, called *Kykeon*.

> It was not lawful, she said for her to drink red wine. She asked them to mix barley meal and water with soft mint and gave her that instead.

> So Meaneira mixed the Kykeon, as she was told to, and offered the cup to the Goddess. And the great queen Deo accepted it for the sake of the rite.[28]

The rites themselves were of an egalitarian nature – anyone who spoke Greek could be initiated into the mysteries of Eleusis if they were not guilty of the shedding of blood. Though the myth is heavily saturated with feminine symbolism, males also initiated into the cult of the Goddess.[29] In Syracuse, at the shrine of Demeter and Persephone, men took the great oath clad in the purple robes of the Goddess and with her burning torch in their hands. Plutarch's *Dion* describes this as the garb of the *mystagogos*, the master of initiation. The same mysteries existed in the Arcadian Pheneos as in Eleusis, and there the priest wore the mask of Demeter Kidaria in the "greatest

[28] CASHWOOD, J., N. & RICHARDSON, N., *The Homeric Hymns*, 14

[29] JUNG, C. G., & KERÉNYI, C., *Essays on a Science of Mythology*, 138

mystery."[30] These rites were strongly associated with the world of Hades, as is illustrated by a passage involving the hero Hercules.

> Having traveled to the land of the dead, Hercules, the archetypal hero, makes a novel suggestion: "Lock up Eleusis and the sacred fire," he says. Thus he purposes to put an end to what Cicero called the best of all "excellent and indeed divine institutions that Athens has brought forth and contributed to human life." It is not, however, that Hercules does not acknowledge the intrinsic value of the mysteries, but through his ultimate experience it seems the hero has found the very pattern upon which the Eleusinian mysteries are based: 'I have experienced far truer mysteries […] I have seen Kore."[31]

This statement by Hercules is recorded on a second century papyrus found in Egyptian Tebtunis, and is also reflected in Euripides fifth century BCE tragedy *Hercules*. Here, too, the hero succeeds in his journey to the land of the dead, but only because he has previously gone through the rites of Eleusis.[32]

In contrast to the depictions of the Underworld in Christian mythos in which the Underworld is largely

---

[30] JUNG, C. G., & KERÉNYI, C., *Essays on a Science of Mythology*, 138

[31] ENDSJO, D. O., To Lock Up Eleusis: A Question of Liminal Space in *Numen*, Vol. 47 (Netherlands: Brill, 2000), 352

[32] Ibid., 353

represented by the element of fire, in the Hellenic Tradition Hades resembles a dark, empty, void. There is a constant sensation of immateriality and inspatiality in Hades, which differs from the physics of the mortal world. This quality of non-existence was also reflected in a sensation of timelessness in Hades, as is indicated by the "psyche of the dead"—or more precisely—the immaterial form of the dead remained forever in the state that it was at the final moment the soul became transposable to Hades.[33]

Evans suggests that "Altars were absent from the interior of the sanctuary because the Mysteries entailed a more egalitarian experience of the Gods than did the traditional customs of *thusia*."[34] However, it also quite likely that altars were absent *because they were not required*. From what is known of the rites, there is an indication that they were more aligned with direct experience of the numinous than with worship. If so, altars would not be a necessary feature. Rather, what seems more likely is that it involved the use of sacred space.

Sacred space falls under the rubric of liminal ritual experiences, because the empty space itself is the focal point of the ritual. The space is referred to as liminal because it is a transition point between the Underworld domain of Hades and that of the world Demeter. Thus, it becomes a ritual threshold for the

33 ENDSJO, D. O., To Lock Up Eleusis: A Question of Liminal Space in *Numen*, Vol. 47, 362

34 EVANS, N. A., Sanctuaries, Sacrifices, and the Eleusinian Mysteries in *Numen*, Vol.49, 227

living to interact with the dead. This corresponds with the eschatia, which represented an area within the ancient Greek world-view that reflected a territorial parallel to the intermediate state of the Greek rites of passage.[35] The Greek eschatia, therefore, becomes the spatial reflection of the interstructural or liminal period a person goes through at the point of dying.[36] For example, Homer and Apollonius of Rhodes respectively had the Odyssean and the Argonautic crew, at the moment when they considered themselves to be lost forever in the liminal space of the eschatia, imitate the ritual drawing of a veil over one's head. This was also enacted at the moment of death by Hippolytus and Socrates. Also, Alcestis, when she returned from the dead, would keep herself covered with a veil. This custom was, moreover, connected to initiatory rites. Just as Demeter would sit with a veil over her face, the neophytes would do this also, imitating the Goddess.[37] The head of the initiate was wrapped in darkness just as in antiquity brides and those vowed to the Underworld were veiled.[38] Accordingly, Sophocles calls those who have reached the *telos* in Eleusis and seen it "thrice happy", saying that "for them alone is there life in death; for the rest, Hades is fell joyless".[39]

---

[35]   ENDSJO, D. O., To Lock Up Eleusis: A Question of Liminal Space in *Numen*, Vol.47, 351

[36]   Ibid., 363

[37]   Ibid., 364

[38]   JUNG, C. G., & KERÉNYI, C., *Essays on a Science of Mythology*, 139.

[39]   Ibid., 144

Far from being a captive, during her time in Hades, Persephone reigns as a queen beside her husband Hades. She even plants a sacred grove beside the River Kokytos (The Lamented) with black poplars and sterile willow trees, on the edge of the realm.[40] The symbolism of the trees is significant, for the black poplar is specifically a 'funeral tree'. Many cultures used their wood to make coffins or masks to decorate the corpses. The sound of poplar leaves rustling in the wind was also believed to send messages to spirits. Poplars were sacred to several other lunar Goddesses, such as Hekate.

In Persephone's role as the Queen of the Underworld, the Sirens, the daughters of Chthon, were her companions, and it was Persephone who sent them to the world of men.[41] Despite her dominion, however, Persephone still pines for the world above ground and the company of her mother. Eventually, her mother Demeter negotiates a bargain for Persephone's release so that they could be reunited. It is agreed that Hades will allow Persephone to leave, under the stipulation that she has not partaken of any food during her time in the Underworld. Unfortunately, prior to leaving, Persephone had consumed pomegranate seeds, (the amount of which varies in different versions of the myth).

---

[40] KERÉNYI, C., *Gods of the Greeks*, 247

[41] Ibid., 58

The eyebrows of Hades were raised in a smile. He was obedient to King Zeus, and at once spoke to his wife: "Go thou, Persephone to thy mother, the Goddess with the dark rainment, go with a gracious heart and be no more exceedingly sad. I shall be no unworthy husband of thee amongst the immortals – am I not own brother to Father Zeus? If perchance thou comest here at times, thou shalt rule over all living creatures and shalt have the greatest honor amongst the Gods. Whoever insulteth thee, and bringeth no sacrifice of contribution, shall atone for it for all eternity."[42]

The fact which it is the pomegranate fruit that binds Persephone to Hades is not coincidental. During

Marble relief, Persephone and Hades 4th century BCE, Eleusis

---

[42] KERÉNYI, C., *The Gods of the Greeks* (UK: Thames & Hudson, 1961), 239

the preparation of funeral feasts, the Greeks did not consume pomegranate, and the fruit was considered to be impure. The fruit was also believed to be a symbol of fertility and/or an aphrodisiac in many cultures, due to the red seeds and the womb-like interior. Likewise, the pomegranate is also a symbol of marriage and is sometimes depicted in the hands of the Goddess Hera. By partaking of the pomegranate with Hades, Persephone is symbolically impregnated by Hades and thus bound to him as his queen. Because of her consumption of the pomegranate seed(s), Persephone could spend two parts of the year with her mother and the rest of the immortals, as is stated here.

> But if you eat anything you will have to go back again to the secret depths of the earth and live there for a third part of the seasons of the year but for the other two parts you will be with me and the other immortals.[43]

Given the narrative of the myth, it is immediately obvious that Persephone's period of reign in Hades corresponds exactly to the time upon the earth in which plant life lies dormant underground during winter. The evidence seems to point towards not a solar myth, but the theft of plant life from the earth. Demeter herself represents the bountiful harvest of the earth, and Persephone is also connected with plants. She is

---

[43] CASHWOOD, J., & RICHARDSON, N., *The Homeric Hymns*, 22

abducted from a field of flowers, and even in Hades she plants a grove of trees. What is depicted at Eleusis is the life and death of the seasons, incorporating the life cycles of both mother and daughter.

As the anthropomorphization of plant life, Persephone reigns as the bride of Hades when the crops wither and winter approaches, when life, invisible and indiscernible to the mortal eye, disappears from the earth to lie dormant beneath the soil awaiting rebirth in spring. Persephone is, therefore, the natural bride for Hades, since each winter she is predestined to die and enter the chthonic realm. Eleusis, with its purpose of being a liminal threshold space for communicating with the realm of the dead, was not a place of death but of rebirth; it was the place for rediscovering Persephone – the eternal maiden, and spirit of life.

DIVINATION,
ONEIROMANCY,
&
NECROMANCY

DIVINATION

THE MANTIC TRADITION

An omen makes it possible to tell what will be one's lot – loss or gain; joy, sorrow, or unalloyed misfortune; long life or death; and the realization of one's wishes and endeavors. When two armies are locked in battle, it can tell which will win the undisputed victory, which will deal the crushing blow.[1]

DIVINATION, OMENS, AND PROPHECIES CAN be referred to as belonging to the Mantic Tradition. Principally concerned with omens, portents, and oracles, these ritual specialists were the seers and diviners of the ancient world. The belief that omens and portents foretell the future through natural phenomenon is ancient and primordial. It still survives today in practices such as astrology, palmistry, tarot cards, and even the reading of tea leaves. Omens such as the behavior of

---

[1] WHITE, D. G., Predicting the Future with Dogs in *Religions of India in Practice* (USA: Princeton University Press,1995), 294

animals and the weather, predate these techniques. A fraction of this lost art exists persists in modern revivals of folklore. Augury is specifically concerned with the study of omens and portents in the natural world, which are deemed to contain signals from the Gods of forthcoming events. Predictions of the future obtained through the divination of omens should not be confused with superstition, however, which is not provided by ritual specialists. Divination via omens and portents is an active process, in which signals from the Gods are deliberately sought – a superstition is passive, and occurs with no active intent on the part of humans. These events are portents because they are deemed to arise from a non-human origin. The study of omens was regarded as a science and its practitioners were accorded the highest degrees of wealth and power by their peers. The lost practices of the mantic tradition and the science of divination once ruled the world and the hearts of our ancestors.

One particular form of divination which has persisted well into the modern era, and even into the sciences via psychology, is dream interpretation, or more correctly, oneiromancy. One specific example of a oneiromantic text from India that survives in full can be found within what is collectively known as the "Six Rites", which is part of the magico-religious practices of Tantrism and the *Mantramahodadhi*, a Hindu treatise on magic. The text describes a list of auspicious (good) and inauspicious (bad) omens. To receive a dream containing an auspicious omen is an indication that if the ritual is performed it will be a success. The revelation of an inauspicious omen in the dream is an indication that Shiva has denied the success of the rite and if it is performed the practitioner will be cursed and will generate negative karmic action. Given the nature of the magic contained within the Six Rites, it is necessary to place this limitation upon its practice, as four of the forms of magic contained within can be easily be described as what is commonly referred to as 'black magic'. The role of the guru is also important for offering advice on how to interpret omens and portents for the dreamer.

The Hellenic world and Mesopotamia also held omens and divination in high regard and it is from these regions that the majority of records on divination originate. The Mantic Tradition held great power within the Mediterranean and the Middle East, with soothsayers and seers to found within the courts of every kingdom. The sibyls and oracles of Rome and Greece utilized trance methods to procure their remarkable visions, which differ in technique from the science of omens that predicts the future from naturally occurring phenomenon and not the production of altered mental states, as was employed by the sibyls and oracles.

Omen texts and inscriptions, such as the *Enuma Anu-enlil* series are believed to go back to the third millennium BCE in view of the references to the fourfold division of the world into the lands of Akkad, Elam, Subartu, and Amurru, and to early kings like Rimush and Ibn-sin.[2] Similarly, in the Sumerian

---

[2]   JAMES, E. O., *The Ancient Gods: The History and Diffusion of*

version of the flood story Ziusudra, or Ut-Napishtim, the Babylonian Noah, is represented as resorting to divinatory practices, and one of the kings of this age, Enmeduranki of Sippur, was alleged to have obtained from the Gods the arts and insignia of divination.[3] From this point of origin the science of omens in the ancient Middle East progressed down many different paths; the Akkadian *barû* (a seer) studied oracles, dreams, and visions, they read omens in the movement of water (hydromancy), the behavior of oil (lecanomancy), celestial phenomenon, and the actions of animals—they also begun to practice what is seen today as a peculiar and barbaric technique— divination by reading the liver of a sacrificial animal (hepatoscopy). This form of divination is particularly difficult for us to comprehend in the modern era, yet to the ancient barû there was a justification for this form of augury. The liver and entrails of the animal were believed to be the core of the animal's soul, and by reading the interior marks and blemishes on the sacrificial animals 'soul' the barû received insights into future events. Also, in Stoic theory, the internal organs were a microcosm of the universe itself, and according to this hypothesis, a detailed examination of the liver (which was believed to be the most important bodily organ) could reveal the future. At any rate, the practice of hepatoscopy spread from the Middle East through to the Etruscan diviners known as haruspices, and from there expanded into the

---

Religion in the Ancient Near East and the Eastern Mediterranean, (London: Readers Union Ltd, 1962), 232

[3]   Ibid.

Greco-Roman world.[4]

Another form of divination which is found in both the Mediterranean traditions and the practices of the barû is a type of divination that is called dream incubation. This type of dream frequently appears in texts of the ancient near east as a substitute term for dream incubation. By stressing the importance of the location in which the dream is experienced, the 'message dream' is closely linked to the incubation dream, as the location is a requirement for both types to successfully induce the dream. To the Greeks, the method of incubation was based on the assumption that the *daimōn*, which was only visible in the higher state achieved by the soul in dreams, had his permanent dwelling at the seat of his oracle.[5] The selection of the space in which to provide dream incubation was of paramount importance. This particular form of divination was sometimes also incorporated with the healing of the sick, and in Greece, it is found in the cult of the healer God Asklepios. One of the Epidaurian inscriptions reports an incident in which a man whose fingers were paralyzed had a dream that he was playing dice, and just when he was about to make a throw the God suddenly appeared, jumped on his hand and stretched out his fingers and straightened them one by one. As

---

[4] JAMES, E. O., *The Ancient Gods: The History and Diffusion of Religion in the Ancient Near East and the Eastern Mediterranean*, 233

[5] ROHDE, E., *Psyche: The Cult of Souls and Belief in Immortality Among the Greeks Vol. 1*, (New York: Harper Torchbooks, 1996), 92

the day dawned, he left the temple cured, although at first, he had doubted the accounts of the cures he had read on the tablets in the precincts of the sanctuary.[6] Although the cult of Asklepios eventually also spread to Rome, in the form of the *Aesculapium*, prior to this divination amongst the Romans was focused on the reading of omens via the natural world, such as the flight of birds or the behavior of lightening. Roman religion was focused on the belief that the divine will could be ascertained from signs and omens that occurred naturally, but in the form of extraordinary phenomena. This idea is again connected to Stoicism, which held that the universe was composed of a fiery spirit that permeated everything (human beings were part of it just as much as birds or cows) and that this rational spirit ordained and controlled everything which happened.[7] One of the official forms of divination in Rome came from the observance of birds.

> In Rome there was a special site (the auguraculum) on the Capital which was reserved for the purpose and the magistrate would be accompanied by one of the colleges of fifteen augurs, distinguished figures like himself, who pronounced the ceremonial formula for designating the quarter of the sky and would interpret, blind-folded, any signs which the magistrate reported. The practice

[6] ROHDE, E., *Psyche: The Cult of Souls and Belief in Immortality Among the Greeks Vol. 1*, 241

[7] OGILVIE, R. M., *The Romans and Their Gods* (UK: Pimlico, 2000), 54.

was regarded so seriously that when in 99 BCE. T. Claudius Centumalus built a house which obstructed the view from the auguraculum he was forced to pull it down.[8]

The practice was not limited to wild birds, for like their Hindu counterparts, the Romans saw the benefits in keeping domesticated livestock for the purposes of divination. Specially raised chickens known as *pullarii* were one of the preferred divinatory tools of augury for the Romans, especially when on military expeditions as the birds could be transported easily. Another method of reading omens which are found amongst the Romans is divination through lightening, which naturally was assumed to reflect the direct will of Jupiter, the king of the Gods who ruled over the sky.

The place where lightening struck was immediately declared holy because it seemed that Jupiter had claimed it for himself. The area, called bidental, was enclosed and sacrifices and prayers were made there. [...] Thunder was also studied. There survives, at third hand, a calendar which gives the significance of thunder-claps on each day of the year. Thus if it thunders on 3 December a shortage of fish will make people eat meat; if it thunders on 19th August, women and slaves will commit murder.[9]

---

[8]   OGILVIE, R. M., *The Romans and Their Gods*, 56

[9]   Ibid., 59

Because the Mantic Tradition was widespread through the Middle East and the Mediterranean regions, we can find many records of its presence, diligently preserved by classical scholars and archaeologists. When it comes to studying the science of omens in the European Traditions, however, the task becomes significantly more difficult due to the gradual erosion of the native European traditions by Christianity over many hundreds of years. The reconstruction of indigenous beliefs is a challenging task, compounded by the lack of research on this aspect of history. Whilst it is widely known that both trance work and runes were employed as divinatory techniques in Europe and Great Britain, the ritual and religious practices of these peoples have not been studied in the same manner as those of Greece, Rome, and the Middle East. Therefore, there is little conclusive evidence as to how and what techniques were actually used for divination. Despite this, we can still find instances of divination via omens and portents in the European traditions. A Gaelic rite of divination called *taghairn* was practiced in the following manner:

> A man is wrapt in the warm skin of an animal just killed, he is then lain down beside a waterfall in the forest, and left alone; by the roar of the waves, it is thought, the future is revealed to him.[10]

---

[10] GRIMM, J., *Teutonic Mythology, Volume III* (USA: Dover Publications, 2004), 1115

Like the Indians, the Teutons had complex systems for reading omens from the behavior of animals; their system differs, however, in that rather than recommending domestic livestock as the ideal candidates for ritual divination and oracular readings, the Teutons deemed domesticated animals unsuitable for the purposes of augury. In this regard, they differed from the Greeks and Romans and there are few instances of birds being used for divination, despite the fact the birds were thought to be messengers of the Gods and heralds of important tidings in the Northern mysteries.[11] Birds that were studied for signs of omens and portents were frequently birds of prey. Ravens and crows also held a position of prominence. In the same manner as the Romans, the Teutons had provided special titles and authority to diviners. In the old Germanic language, we find the words *heilisôn, heilisôd, heilisari,* and *heilisara,* which are all equivalents to the term augury.[12]

> The sacred priestly tradition appears, like the priestly office itself, to have been hereditary in families. A female fortune-teller declared that the gift had long been in her family, and on her death would descend to her eldest daughter: from mother to daughter therefore, and from father to son; by some it is maintained that soothsaying and the gift of healing must be handed down from women to men, from men to women.[13]

---

[11]   Ibid., 11128

[12]   Ibid., 11106

[13]   GRIMM, J., *Teutonic Mythology, Volume III,* 11107

The art of divination was at one time employed by all the major civilizations of the ancient world, and its techniques were as varied as its practice was widespread. The practitioners of this ancient art were accorded with titles and rank, sometimes with power so great their prophecies and predictions shaped the destinies of empires and the tides of battle. Although their techniques may seem unusual, we must ask ourselves if such practices could still be relevant today. With our contemporary knowledge of science and advanced understanding of man's role in the natural world, we are once again progressing towards a sense of unity with nature; we are no longer in opposition to the will of the earth. We are learning not to pillage her harvests and are restoring the precocious balance between civilization and nature – this is what our ancient ancestors already understood by reading the actions of animals. Animals have not lost their natural instincts which tie them closely to the environment in which they live – in humanity this instinct is subdued. There are few biologists who would doubt that an animal can foretell the weather or natural events better than a human, and it is precisely for this reason that our ancestors chose to rely upon the study of natural phenomenon for the science of divination; what they were reading was the will of nature, which in many ways is a direct experience of the will of the Gods.

ONEIROMANCY
&
NECROMANCY

DEAD BUT DREAMING
ONEIROMANCY & NECROMANCY IN HELLENIC
TRADITION

That is not dead which can eternal lie / And with strange aeons even Death may die.

– H. P. Lovecraft

THE GREATEST MYSTERIES DO NOT lie within the depths of space or the fathomless oceans; rather they remain in the uncharted regions of the mind, forever out of reach, dwelling at the point where our capacity for conscious thought ceases. In sleep and in death, we know very little of what occurs – both remain shrouded in darkness and lay beyond the empirical boundaries of modern science. Curiously, the more primitive and ancient a society is, the greater it's understanding of the ambiguities contained by dreams and death. Traditional cultures possessed a far greater understanding of death and the dying process than that of the people in the modern West, where we dwell in comfort, keeping ourselves isolated from all things harmful and intrusive to the psyche.

Hellenic Tradition and classical myth will reveal more about the nature of consciousness and how dreams and death are connected than any contemporary work on psychology could offer. Likewise, the Hellenic tradition will also explain how these are linked by the concept of the soul, and also how the diviners and magicians devised mechanisms to exploit these techniques in the world of the occult, primarily via the two esoteric schools which would eventually come to be known as oneiromancy and necromancy.

ONEIROMANCY

I had a dream, which was not all a dream.

– Lord Byron, *Darkness*

Since the dawn of time when the very first tendrils of consciousness began to unfurl in the recesses of the mind, humans have led a seemingly dualistic existence, torn between the world of daylight and the nocturnal world of dreams. Sometimes profoundly beautiful and at other times terrifying, dreams have captivated the minds of some of our greatest thinkers, representing an object of wonder to them, vibrant and potent with mystery. In the ancient world, they were deeply associated with religious experience and regarded as messages from the divine. It is this prophetic aspect that makes the dream such a powerful divinatory tool to ascertain future events. As an aspect of being which has no tautologically verifiable status and cannot be empirically measured, the phenomenon of dreams sits in a category of consciousness which at the present time cannot been adequately explained. However, when examined with appropriate discernment, it can be seen that its existence is not purely contingent with the faculties normally associated with a corporeal form, and whether illusory or not, this is indicative of an alteration in cognition at the very least.

Dreams were employed for specific goals such as prophecy, divination, or producing an epiphany, which was referred to as oneiromancy. The only fully surviving Greek text on oneiromancy is the *Oneirocritica* of Artemidorus of Daldis, and even this is only partially translated into English. Though dated to a relatively late period in the second century CE, the *Oneirocritica* nevertheless represents the pinnacle of a long oneiromantic tradition, in which Artemidorus himself cites numerous other dream interpreters and their works by name.[1]

The *Oneirocritica,* as a text, strives to remain remarkably rational in its approach to dream analysis. Artemidorus argued that the dreamer's occupation, habits, and attitudes must all be taken into account before any dream could be interpreted, and like many

---

[1] NOEGEL, S. B., ed. PETTINATO, G. P., *Dreaming and the Ideology of Mantics: Homer and Ancient Near Eastern Oneiromancy* (USA: Proceedings of the Third Annual Symposium of the Assyrian and Babylonian Intellectual Heritage Project, 2000), 170

modern dream interpreters, Artemidorus noted that many dreams were simply a continuation of the prior day's activities and possessed no divinatory meaning. Therefore, not all dreams were deemed to be lucrative for the purpose of divination. A well-known passage from the *Aeneid* also explains that not all dreams have prophetic value. The *Aeneid* states that there are two types of dreams – those from the Gate of Horn, and those from the Gate of Ivory. Only those from the Gate of Horn are prophetic in nature.

> "Dreams, my friend," said the thoughtful Penelope, "are awkward and confusing things: not all that people see in them comes true. For there are two gates through which these unsubstantial visions reach us; one is of horn and the other of ivory. Those that come through the carved ivory gate deceive/harm us bringing unfulfilment; whereas those that issue from the gate of burnished horn really fulfill."[2]

The topic of oneiromancy was one the Greeks took very seriously, and the study of oneiromancy was by no means restricted to just Artemidorus. References to oneiromancy appear in the works of well-known authors such as Plato, Homer, and Aristotle. Aristotle devoted two short treatises to the subject, *De Insomniis* (*On Dreams*) and *De Divinatione per Somnum* (*On Prophesying by Dreams*), in which he

[2] NOEGEL, S. B., ed. PETTINATO, G. P., *Dreaming and the Ideology of Mantics: Homer and Ancient Near Eastern Oneiromancy*, pp. 176-177

analyzed the basic features of sleep and dreaming, and explained them in terms of the natural laws of physics.[3] On the topic of interpreting dreams, Aristotle says that,

> The most skillful interpreter of dreams is he who has the faculty of observing resemblances. Anyone may interpret dreams which are vivid and plain. But, speaking of 'resemblances', I mean that dream presentations are analogous to the forms reflected in water, as indeed we have already stated. In the latter case, if the motion in the water is great, the reflexion has no resemblance to its original, nor do the forms resemble the real objects. Skillful, indeed, would he be in interpreting such reflexions who could rapidly discern, and at a glance comprehend, the scattered and distorted fragments of such forms, so as to perceive that one of them represents a man, or a horse, Or anything whatever. Accordingly, in the other case also, in a similar way, some such thing as this [blurred image] is all that a dream amounts to; for the internal movement effaces the clearness of the dream.[4]

Aristotle, though known for his application of scientific method, nonetheless does accept the

[3] BULKELEY, K., *Dreaming in the World's Religions* (USA: NYU Press, 2008), 157

[4] ARISTOTLE, trans. BEARE, J. L., *On Prophesying by Dreams,* http://classics.mit.edu/Aristotle/prophesying.html

validity of prophetic dreams and accepts them as a natural part of the dreaming process. In this regard, much of his hypothesis appears to be derived from the writing of Democritus, from whom he derives his explanation of the event as a form of 'temporal echoing' of a future event. What is especially interesting in this next passage is that Aristotle does not ascribe the ability to detect this to the intelligent, but to people who are "commonplace and not the most intelligent". According to Aristotle, their minds are less likely to be "active" at night and more receptive to these prophetic vibrations. This is an interesting theory, despite questionable logic on Aristotle's part to associate receptive ability with a lack of intelligence.

> As for [prophetic] dreams which involve not such beginnings [sc. of future events] as we have here described, but such as are extravagant in times, or places, or magnitudes; or those involving beginnings which are not extravagant in any of these respects, while yet the persons who see the dream hold not in their own hands the beginnings [of the event to which it points]: unless the foresight which such dreams give is the result of pure coincidence, the following would be a better explanation of it than that proposed by Democritus, who alleges 'images' and 'emanations' as its cause. As, when something has caused motion in water or air, this [the portion of water or air], and, though the cause has ceased to operate, such motion propagates itself to a certain

point, though there the prime movement is not present; just so it may well be that a movement and a consequent sense-perception should reach sleeping souls from the objects from which Democritus represents 'images' and 'emanations' coming; that such movements, in whatever way they arrive, should be more perceptible at night [than by day], because when proceeding thus in the daytime they are more liable to dissolution (since at night the air is less disturbed, there being then less wind); and that they shall be perceived within the body owing to sleep, since persons are more sensitive even to slight sensory movements when asleep than when awake. It is these movements then that cause 'presentations', as a result of which sleepers foresee the future even relatively to such events as those referred to above. *These considerations also explain why this experience befalls commonplace persons and not the most intelligent.* For it would have regularly occurred both in the daytime and to the wise had it been God who sent it; but, as we have explained the matter, it is quite natural that commonplace persons should be those who have foresight [in dreams]. For the mind of such persons is not given to thinking, but, as it were, derelict, or totally vacant, and, when once set moving, is borne passively on in the direction taken by that which moves it. With regard to the fact that some persons who are liable to derangement have this foresight, its explanation is that their normal mental movements do not impede [the alien movements], but are beaten off by the latter. Therefore it is that they have an especially keen perception of the alien movements.[5]

What Aristotle means in terms of the passivity of the mind and its receptivity to these emanations which may foretell of future events, is that some individuals can alter their brain wave patterns when in a relaxed state. For example, theta and delta waves are active during the brain in sleep cycles, and there are possibly more that have not yet been discovered. Intelligence, which tends to be a more active faculty of conscious thought, could interfere with a passive or receptive mode of consciousness. These individuals may not be 'commonplace' at all, but could be able to reduce external noise down and filter it out somehow so that the brain is more receptive to prophetic dreaming. This would require a type of altered consciousness, which maybe why Aristotle also associates it with a 'vacant' state and 'derangement' in individuals who are deemed to be true prophetic dreamers. It would therefore not be a matter of intelligence of all, but rather an application of a different type of cognitive ability which is rarely found—even less so when coupled with coherence—in which case it is incorrect for Aristotle to base it on intelligence alone. Clearly, however, oneiromancy did sometimes require the induction of an altered state of consciousness which not all people were capable of having, and that this

---

[5] ARISTOTLE, trans. BEARE, J. I., *On Prophesying by Dreams By Aristotle*

was not entirely restricted to the stupid and the mad, as Aristotle would have us believe.

In some sources, the Greeks use the word "to see" to describe a dream experience, indicating that the prophetic dream was perceived to be more vivid than a normal dream. Oneiromancy was a very cryptic process which required specialist interpretation. As for the techniques used to decipher dreams, three main methodologies appear to have been used – *gematria* (assigning a numerical value to words & numbers), *polysemy* (different but related meanings) and *paranomasia* (wordplay or rhetoric). Examples of each type are described here.

A weasel that appears in a dream represents a lawsuit, since both words, when treated as numbers, equal forty-two (3 + 1 + 30 + 8 = 42/ 4 + 10 +20 + 8 = 42) (gematria).[6]

A penis in a dream can signify the making of important plans (polysemy).[7]

A wolf signifies a year because of its name (paronomasia).[8]

[6]   NOEGEL, S. B., ed. PETTINATO, G. P., *Dreaming and the Ideology of Mantics: Homer and Ancient Near Eastern Oneiromancy,* 30

[7]   Ibid., 31

[8]   Ibid.

Part of the popularity of Hellenic oneiromancy arises from contact with adjacent cultures in the Middle East. Both Walter Burkert and Fritz Graf attribute an influence to Near Eastern mantic culture, which accelerated the spread of interest in divination throughout the Homeric West.[9] This is immediately apparent in *The Greek Magical Papyri*, where not only is there a request for a dream oracle cited, but also numerous references to Egyptian sources which occur throughout the entire text.

VIII. REQUEST FOR A DREAM ORACLE

Take a strip of clean linen and write on it the following name. Roll it up to make a wick, pour pure olive oil over it and light it.

The formula to be written is this: "HARMIOUTH LAILAM CHO'OUCH ARSENOPHRE' PHRE'U PHTHA HARCHENTECHTHA."

In the evening then, when you are about to go to sleep, being pure in every respect, do this: go to the lamp, say seven times the following formula, extinguish the light and go to sleep.

The Formula to be spoken is as follows: "SACHMOUNE [i.e., Sakhmet] PAE'MALIGOTE'RE'E'NCH, the one who shakes,

---

[9] NOEGEL, S. B., ed. PETTINATO, G. P., *Dreaming and the Ideology of Mantics: Homer and Ancient Near Eastern Oneiromancy*, 180

GWENDOLYN TAUNTON

who thunders, who has swallowed the serpent, surrounds the moon, and hour by hour raises the disk of the Sun, CHTHETHO'NI is Your Name. I ask You, Lords of the Gods, SE'TH CHRE'PS: reveal to me concerning the Things I wish."[10] [PGM VII. 359-69]

These practices were widely known throughout the ancient world. In some cases, there is even continuity of the practice in medieval Europe. Dream incubation, for example, which entails a direct contact with the divine, exists as a separate branch within the broader application of oneiromancy. In dream incubation, ritual sleep is deliberately induced by the practitioner with the sole purpose of inducing vivid dreams that would reveal wisdom, or enable the dreamer to serve as an oracle.[11] The use of dream incubation here is also translates into a cultic term or phrase in various languages, with very specific fields of meaning – one example of this can be seen in the Ancient Greek word *enkamexis*, which means sleeping in a sanctuary.[12] Likewise, the Latin etymology implies the action of lying down, and gestating in the dark,

---

[10]   BETZ, H. D., (ed.), *The Greek Magical Papyri in Translation Including the Demotic Spells* (USA: The University of Chicago Press, 1986), [PGM IV. 1323-30]

[11]   PATTERN, K. C., "A Great and Strange Correction:" Intentionality, Locality, and Epiphany in the Category of Dream Incubation in *History of Religions,* vol. 43, No. 3 (USA: University of Chicago Press,2004), 197

[12]   Ibid., 201.

characteristically in a small enclosed space.[13] This form of oneiromantic dream induction is also known as the 'message' dream, which is experienced after due preparation within the God's sanctuary.[14]

In regard to message dreams, there is also an association of dreams with the Underworld. This occurs in Homer's *Odyssey* (24: 11-12) in which the souls of the dead are taken by Hermes past the Gates of Helios and the Land of Dreams.[15] There is a distinction between message dreams and symbolic dreams, which includes the *topos* of a dream figure standing by the head of one's bed, and a preoccupation with the time in which a dream occurs.[16] Message dreams frequently appear in texts from the ancient Near East as a substitute for dream incubation. By stressing the importance of the location in which the dream is experienced, the message dream is thus closely linked to incubation dreams, since the location is one of the main requirements for successfully inducing a message dream.

The locations for dream incubation are closely identified with their respective Gods, and some are believed to be inhabited by the God's presence.

---

[13] PATTERN, K. C., "A Great and Strange Correction:" Intentionality, Locality, and Epiphany in the Category of Dream Incubation in *History of Religions*, vol. 43, No. 3, 196

[14] BREMMER., J., *The Early Greek Concept of the Soul*, (USA: Princeton University, 1983), 20

[15] NOEGEL, S. B., ed. PETTINATO, G. P., *Dreaming and the Ideology of Mantics: Homer and Ancient Near Eastern Oneiromancy*, 170

[16] Ibid.

Because a God 'inhabits' the area, this place is the one where a dream is most likely to be granted by the God. Accordingly, incubated dreams are referred to as God-sent (*theopemti*).[17]

For the Greeks, the method of incubation was based on the assumption that the *daimōn*, was only visible in a higher state of perception, and permanently dwelt beside his or her oracle.[18] The selection of the space in which to practice dream incubation was therefore of paramount importance. The preparation for sleeping in such an area is also a ritual act, equivalent to any other ceremony in its contribution to the sacred.

Dream incubation could not occur anywhere — it had to occur at a specific location. The notion of a geographic location existing as an axis between two worlds—that of the Gods and that of the mortals—is by no means restricted to the practice of dream incubation. This idea is frequently cited by authors such as Mircea Eliade, as the 'sacred center'. Furthermore, it can be seen in sites which still exist today that are believed to act as cosmic *foci* for special rites. Such locales where special formations of the earth were connected with ritual activities were called *kratophanies* by Eliade. This idea is especially pertinent to the topic of dream incubation, because

[17] PATTERN, K. C., "A Great and Strange Correction:" Intentionality, Locality, and Epiphany in the Category of Dream Incubation in *History of Religions*, vol. 43, No. 3, 205

[18] ROHDE, E., *Psyche: The Cult of Souls and Belief in Immortality among the Greeks Vol I* (USA: Harper Torchbooks, 1996), 92

the practice is usually connected to chthonic deities. In the case of figures such as Amphiaros and Trophanos, though they are not explicitly chthonic, they receive the same sacrifices as Gods that dwell within the earth, and the effectiveness of aid sought from the two entities is directly linked to their locale.[19] Amphiaros only revealed the future to those who slept in his temple, and to question Trophonios one first had to pass through a narrow passage into his cave.[20]

In ancient Greek religion, the earth is sometimes referred to as a Goddess, who was also believed to engender dreams. This is amply illustrated in Euripides' *Hecuba* when the wife of King Priam addresses the earth at line 70.

> *O Potnia Chthon, melanon pterugon meter oneiron*
> (O Lady Earth, mother of black winged dreams).[21]

An important distinction to make here is the usage of the term *chthon* instead of the word *ge*. Chthon translates as 'underworld' whereas ge translates as 'underground' - hence the two words do not relate to the same plane of existence. Ge lies beneath the earth on which we stand upon as a physical and corporeal fact, and chthon exists below this world, referring to a metaphysical or ontological concept which alludes to another plane of existence. As such, the term chthon

---

[19] ROHDE, E., *Psyche: The Cult of Souls and Belief in Immortality among the Greeks Vol. I*, 92

[20] Ibid.

[21] PATTERN, K. C., "A Great and Strange Correction:" Intentionality, Locality, and Epiphany in the Category of Dream Incubation in *History of Religions*, vol. 43, No. 3, 205

can neither be easily translated nor understood without direct experience. The renowned archetypal psychologist Hillman renders the difference betwixt the two as thus:

> Chthon with its derivatives refers in origin to the cold, dead depths and has nothing to do with fertility. This kind of deep ground is not the same as the dark earth, and the Great Lady (*Potnia Chthon*), who sends black-winged dreams and who can also be called Erinyes cannot simply be merged into the single figure of the Great Earth Mother.[22]

> Ge herself shows two aspects. On the one hand, she has to do with retributive justice, with the Fates, and she has also mantic oracular powers, (Ge Chthonia was worshiped on Mykonos, together with Zeus Chthonios and Dionysos Leneus, as she was linked with the chthonic Pluto and Hermes and the Erinyes at Athens [Areopagus].) This is the "Great Lady" who sends the black-winged dreams and is appropriately the mother of Themis ("Justice"). This spiritual side of her can be distinguished, on the other hand, from the physical Ge to whom fruits and grains were given (Ge-Demeter). Demeter too has a mystery aspect; her daughter Persephone belongs to Hades and has an underworld function.[23]

---

[22] HILLMAN, J., *The Dream and the Underworld* (USA: Harper & Row Publishers, 1979), 35
[23] Ibid., 37

The connection between these two titles Chthon and Ge is indicative of an association between the earth, dreams, and the Underworld. This can also be seen in cases from the Near East and Mediterranean regions, wherein Gods sometimes appeared to their worshipers in theriomorphic form. Two prime examples of this are the Greek Gods of healing, Asklepios and Amphiaraios, whom routinely took the form of a great serpent in incubated dreams.[24]

Like his fellow prophet Asclepius, Trophonius appeared to his audience in both human form and in the form of a snake, and *The Suda* informs us that a snake announced the prophecies. Trophonius may have been identified with snakes of the *pareias* family that inhabited his abode, which were also sacred to Asclepius. The honey-barley cakes taken down there were said to be fed to snakes or to Trophonius himself.[25] The keeping and feeding of snakes for ritual purposes was fairly common in the ancient world.

Serpents rank among the oldest and most well-known symbols of the earth. The coiled serpent represents the rotations of the earth, which are found depicted not only as the Ouroboros but also as the Midgard serpent, and in Vedic Tradition. Clearly, as a symbol of time (the rotation of the earth), the role of the serpent in divination and prophecy is an obvious one. Frequently in myth, the serpent is coiled

---

[24] PATTERN, K. C., "A Great and Strange Correction:" Intentionality, Locality, and Epiphany in the Category of Dream Incubation in *History of Religions,* vol. 43, No. 3, 207

[25] OGDEN, D., *Greek and Roman Necromancy* (USA: Princeton University Press, 2001), 84

around an object such as a tree or pillar which bridges the three worlds (heaven, the mortal realm, and the chthonic). In these instances, the serpent is guarding the *axis mundi* of the sacred, protecting it from violation by outsiders.

Of the great oracles, there are none more famous than the Oracle of Delphi. The site itself is built over an older tradition, which was eventually supplanted by the cult of Apollo, and there are many unusual features present at Delphi that are not normally associated with the God. For example, although the Oracle was sacred to Apollo, Dionysus was also worshiped at Delphi. Delphi had a previous legacy of serpent and chthonic based cults, via the myth of Python, the mythological serpent whom the Pythia (priestess) is named after. As time progressed, however, Apollo, as the primary God of divination, quickly became associated with Delphi.

Originally, consultation at Delphi occurred on a single day per year (Apollo's birthday, Bysios 7th, in late February), but by Plutarch's time business was so heavy that two Pythias were in constant operation, all year round (except for the three months Apollo was absent with the Hyperboreans, during which time Dionysus reigned at Delphi).[26]

The Oracle was so well regarded that even Plato accepted the validity of oracles at Delphi (*Rep.* 427bc), along with the oracles of Ammon and Dodona (*Laws.* 787bd and 759de).[27]

---

[26]   STONEMAN, R., *The Ancient Oracles: Making the Gods Speak*, 27

[27]   Ibid., 36

Oracle of Delphi, red-figure *kylix*, 440-430 BCE

Diodorus Siculus, in the *Library of History*, describes the mysterious origin of the Delphi Oracle, writing that,

> It is said that in ancient times goats discovered the oracular shrine, on which account even to this day the Delphians use goats preferably when they consult the oracle. They say that the manner of its discovery was the following. There is a chasm at this place where now is situated what is known as the 'forbidden' sanctuary [the *adyton*], and as goats had been wont to feed about this because

Delphi had not as yet been settled, invariably any goat that approached the chasm and peered into it would leap about in an extraordinary fashion and utter a sound quite different from what it was formerly wont to emit. The herdsman in charge of the goats marveled at the strange phenomenon and having approached the chasm and peeped down into it to discover what it was, has the same experience as the goats, for the goats begun to act like beings possessed and the goatherd also begun to foretell future events. After this the report was bruited among the people of the vicinity concerning the experience of those who approached the chasm, an increasing number of persons visited the place and, as they tested it because of its miraculous character, whosoever approached the spot became inspired. For these reasons, the oracles came to be regarded as a marvel and to be considered the prophecy-giving shrine of Earth. For some time all who wished to obtain a prophecy approached the chasm and made their prophetic replies to one another; but later, since many were leaping down into the chasm under the influence of their frenzy and all disappeared, it seemed best to the dwellers in that region, in order to eliminate the risk, to station one woman there as prophetess for all and to have the oracles told through her. And for her, a contrivance was devised which she could safely mount, then become inspired and give prophecies to those who so desired…It is said that in ancient times virgins delivered the oracles because virgins have their natural innocence intact...(but as a result of the rape of one of these virgins) the Delphians passed a law that in future a virgin should no longer prophesy but that an elderly woman of fifty should declare the oracles and that she should be dressed in the costume of a virgin, as a sort of reminder of the prophetess of olden time.[28]

From this passage it is clear that the origin of Delphi's power is chthonic in origin as it arises from a deep chasm in the earth, and contact with its primordial energy drives both animals and humans alike into a frenzy.

---

[28] STONEMAN, R., *The Ancient Oracles: Making the Gods Speak*, 33

DREAMS AND THE UNDERWORLD

> Never the spirit was born, the spirit shall cease
> to be never. Never was time it was not, end and
> beginning are dreams.
>
> – *Bhagavad Gita*

The association between dreams and the Underworld
is well documented and is widespread across many
cultural groups – it can even be cited in one of the
world's oldest texts, the *Atharva Veda*, wherein it
is stated that dreams originate from the domain
of Yama, the Lord of the Dead. It is for this reason
that the practice of dream divination is performed
whilst facing the South.[29] This close association
between death and dreams is also prevalent in the
Greek mythos. In Homer's *Illiad*, Hypnos (Sleep)
and Thanatos (Death) are twin brothers. Likewise,
Dreams (Oneirori) are mentioned as the children
of Nyx (Night) in Hesiod's *Theogony* and they are
part of her great brood, which also includes Old
Age, Envy, Strife, Doom, Lamentation, Destiny,
and Deceit.[30] Somewhat like Homer's *demos oneiron*,
Hesiod's *Oneiroi* suggested a vague personification of
dreaming, and a tendency to adopt a vaguely human
form, perhaps even to the extent of generating a sense

---

[29] WAYMAN, A., Significance of dreams in India and Tibet in
History of Religions, Vol. 7, No. 1 (USA: University of Chicago
Press, 1967), 6

[30] HILLMAN, J., *The Dream and the Underworld,* 32

Hypnos and Thanatos,
© Marie Lan Nguyen
Wikimedia Commons

of community among the dreams themselves.[31]

Another text which links the world of dreams to that of the dead is the *Pindar Fragment*.

In happy fate all die a death that frees from care. And yet there still will linger behind in
A living image of life,
For this alone lingers with the Gods

It sleeps while the members are active; but to those who sleep themselves
It reveals in myriad visions The fateful approach
Of adversities or delight.[32]

The *Pindar Fragment* alludes to a dualistic consciousness — the *eidolon* (image of life) sleeps when the body is active, but when the body is asleep it can reveal the future via dreams. What is important here is the use of the term 'eidolon' — the eidolon is a mirror image of the physical body. As such, it should be regarded as distinct from the Homeric concept in which different types of souls are named

[31] BULKELEY, K., *Dreaming in the Worlds Religions,* pp. 146-147

[32] BREMMER, J., *The Early Greek Concept of the Soul,* 7

— the free soul, corresponding with the psyche, and bodily souls, which correspond with *thymos, noos,* and *menos*. The eidolon is similar to the concept of an 'astral form' or what is created in esoteric yogic practice as an 'Illusory Body.'

Although the eidolon appears to be different in terminology to the Greek concept of the soul, there are also textual passages that mention the departure of the soul from its material vessel in a similar manner to the nocturnal wanderings of the eidolon. In a text by Xenophon, a similar form of behavior is exhibited by the soul during sleep: "It is in sleep that it enjoys a certain insight into the future, and this apparently, because it is freest in sleep (Xenophon *Cyropaedy* 8.7.21, trans. Dodds).[33]

As with the mystic doctrines concerning 'Illusory Bodies' and 'astral forms', the use of the eidolon also seems to have been deployed in Hellenic magic, and is very similar to what is currently known as 'astral projection', which is also named as one of the eight primary *siddhi* arising from the practice of yoga.[34] This practice involved a lot more than merely sleeping. Some instances involved a ritually enacted trance state in a which a magician's (or their assistant's) soul left their body and entered the world of dreams to divine an answer. A description of this process is found in the journey of Aristeas of Proconnesus, as reported by Maximus of Tyre.

---

[33] BREMMER., J., *The Early Greek Concept of the Soul*, 51

[34] *Prāptisiddhi* (having unrestricted access to all places), which is alternatively named in the *Bhagavata Purana* as *manaḥ-javah*.

As he lay on the ground, scarcely breathing, his soul, abandoning his body, wandered like a bird and saw everything beneath it: earth, sea, rivers, towns, the customs and passions of mankind, and natures of every kind. Then, returning to its body and making it rise, using it once again as an instrument, it told what it had seen and heard.[35]

In another passage, Maximus says that Aristeas' soul, after leaving the body, flew directly towards the *aither*. Aristeas then evidently made his journey to the fantastic lands north of the Black Sea by means of soul-projection. According to Herodotus, Aristeas, who was also known as *phoibolamptos* ('possessed by Apollo'), returned to Proconnesus (situated in the Propontis) after six years in order to write the *Arimaspeia*.[36] Aristeas' reappearance is undated, but even if it occurred at the time of Herodotus' writing, it dates his lifetime to the early seventh century. Aristeas was referred to by Strabo as a sorcerer (*goēs*) *par excellence*.[37]

Similar behavior of the soul during sleep can also be found in the *Eumenides* of Aeschylus where Clytemnestra says "for in sleep the *phren* (mind) is

---

[35] MIHAJ, A., Soul's Aitherial Abode According to the Poteidaia Epitaph and the Presocratic Philosophers in *Numen* 57 (Netherlands: Brill, 2010), 573

[36] Ibid.

[37] OGDEN, J., *Witchcraft and Ghosts in the Greek and Roman Worlds: A Source Book* (UK: Oxford University Press, 2009), 15

lightened."[38] Apollonius also relates the following event in the tale of Hermotimos (*Mirabilia* 3).

> They say that the soul of Hermotimos of Clazomenae, wandering apart from the body, was absent for many years, and in different places foretold events such as great floods and droughts and also earthquakes and plagues and the like, while his stiff body was lying inert, and that the soul, after certain periods, re-entering the body as into a sheath, aroused it. As he did this often, and although his wife had orders from him that, whenever he was going to be in trance (lit. to depart) nobody should touch his 'corpse', neither one of the citizens nor anybody else, some people went into his house and, having moved his weak wife by entreaty, they gazed at Hermotimos lying on the ground, naked and motionless. They took fire and burned him, thinking that the soul, when it should arrive and have no place to enter, would be completely deprived of being alive – which indeed happened. The inhabitants of Clazomenae honor Hermotimos till the present day and a sanctuary for him has been founded into which no woman enters for the reason given.[39]

Tertullian also reports similar events in regards to Hermotimus,

---

[38]   BREMMER., J., *The Early Greek Concept of the Soul*, 51
[39]   Ibid., 27.

With regard to the case of Hermotimus, they say that he used to be deprived of his soul in his sleep as if it wandered away from his body like a person on a holiday trip. His wife betrayed the strange peculiarity. His enemies, finding him asleep, burnt his body as if it were a corpse: when his soul returned too late, it appropriated (I suppose) to itself the guilt of the murder.[40]

The extraction of the soul for divinatory purposes was also performed on others, as well as on the magicians and sorcerers themselves – and these were referred to as *pneumatic experiments*. The preferred medium for these experiments were boys instead of adults, as it was believed that their souls were purer and less rooted in the body. In Plato's dialogue *Meno*, Socrates uses a boy's soul for his demonstration of the theory of knowledge as *anamnesis* or recollection.[41] As for the soul-attracting wand or rod, by means of which one can draw the soul out of the body, Georges Méautis associates it with the staff of Hermes, the guide of souls.[42] Here again, we see the phenomena of oneiromancy connected to the departure of the soul from the body in trance or states of altered consciousness — because this renders the body into

[40] MIHAJ, A., Soul's Aitherial Abode According to the Poteidaia Epitaph and the Presocratic Philosophers in *Numen* 57, 573

[41] Ibid., 572

[42] MIHAJ, A., Soul's Aitherial Abode According to the Poteidaia Epitaph and the Presocratic Philosophers in *Numen* 57, 572

a comatose or cataleptic state which closely resembles death and it frees part of the soul from the body. Both the eidolon and the soul can depart from the body during sleep, trance, or death states. During such cataleptic phenomena, to the casual observer there is little difference between them.

The Land of the Dead and the Land of Dreams are so close that the boundaries between the two divinatory spheres of oneiromancy and necromancy can even be crossed as is seen here, where the ghost of Patroklos appears to Achilles in a dream.

> The ghost came and stood over his head and spoke a word to him: "You sleep, Achilles, you have forgotten me; but you were not careless of me when I lived, but only in death. Bury me as quickly as may be, let me pass through the gates of Hades".[43]

In the dream Achilles promised he would do so, and he asked Patroklos to stay,

> "But stand closer to me, and let us, if only for a little, embrace, and take full satisfaction from the dirge of sorrow." So he [Achilles] spoke, and with his own arms reached for him [Patroklos], but could not take him, but the spirit went underground, like vapor, with a thin cry, and Achilles started awake, staring, and drove his hands together, and spoke, and his words were sorrowful: "Oh, wonder! Even in the house of

---

[43]   BULKELEY, K., *Dreaming in the World's Religions*, 142

Hades there is left something, a soul, and an image, but there is no real heart of life in it."[44]

Even the physical location the Greeks believed dreams to emanate from was located geographically located in the proximity of Hades. The *Odyssey* provides a brief reference to a location for the dream world, where the suitors slaughtered by Odysseus were led by the god Hermes on their final journey.

And Hermes the Healer led them on, and down the dank mouldering paths and past the Ocean's streams they went and past the White Rock and the Sun's Western Gates and past the Land of Dreams (*demos oneiron*), and they soon reached the fields of asphodel where the dead, the burnt-out wraiths of mortals, make their home.[45]

The Land of Dreams, therefore, is located directly adjacent to Hades itself. This leads to an interesting corundum concerning interpretations of the *Odyssey's* Book XI, which is alternately described as a depiction of *katabasis* (descent) to Hades or a description of *nekuia* (necromancy). Homer's *Odyssey* is an epic poem which was transmitted as an oral tradition, and is generally dated around 700-650 BCE. However, because it was an oral tradition no precise date can be accurately set and it could have existed in oral form prior to this date.

---

[44]   BULKELEY, K., *Dreaming in the World's Religions*, 142

[45]   Ibid., pp. 146-147

The *Odyssey* itself can be interpreted as the passage of a solar hero who circumnavigates the globe, only to pass through the dark side/underworld and re-emerge as part of the seasonal cycle. In this light, the descent seems more akin to katabasis, especially since Odysseus is deemed to be physically present in Hades. As for the description of the dead, some are mentioned as having corporeal forms, whilst others, such as his mother, are more intangible. Pausanias seems inclined to accept that it is a depiction of katabasis, for he describes a painting by Polygnotus at Delphi of Odysseus descending into Hades.

The physical location of the entrance to Hades, is mentioned by the *Odyssey* as being near the confluence of the two rivers Acheron and Cocytus.

> Go yourself to the dank house of Hades. There: the Pyriphlegethon and the Cocytus, which is an off-flow of the Styx, flowing into the Acheron, and there is a rock and the confluence: of two loud-thundering rivers. Draw near to there and, as I bid you, dig a trench.[46]

There is also a clear description of nekuia in Book XI, where Odysseus summons the ghost of the seer Tiresias with the aid of Circe.

> Odysseus digs a pit (*bothros*). He pours libations around it to all the dead, first of a mixture of milk and honey, *melikraton*, second of sweet wine, and

---

[46]   OGDEN, D., *Greek and Roman Necromancy,* 46

third of water, and then he sprinkles barley on top.[47] He prays to the dead, promising to sacrifice to all of them on his return home the best sterile heifer of his herd and to burn treasures on a pyre for them. To the ghost of the prophet Tiresias [...] he promises a separate sacrifice of his outstanding all-black ram. With his bronze sword, he opens the necks of (jugulates) a pair of black sheep, male and female, holding their heads down toward the underworld while turning his own face in the opposite direction. He lets their blood flow into the pit. At this point, the ghosts gather. Odysseus orders his companions Perimedes and Eurylochus to flay the sheep and burns their bodies in holocaust (i.e. to burn them whole), and to pray to Hades and Persephone. All the ghosts are eager to drink the blood, which will give them the power of recognition and speech, so Odysseus must use his sword to ensure that only those ghosts with whom he chose to converse approach it. But before he can select and speak to the ghost of Tiresias, he is confronted, unbidden, by that of his dead comrade Elpenor, who asks him to secure his burial.[48]

The actual rituals and locations utilized in necromancy will be presented later. At this point what is important is that in the *Odyssey*, Odysseus passes

[47]   OGDEN, D., *Greek and Roman Necromancy*, XXIII

[48]   Ibid., XIV

through both the Land of Dreams and the Land of the Dead – both of which are in close proximity to each other, indicating the close relationship betwixt the two. It is by katabasis that one *descends* to the Underworld and by nekuia that one *raises* the dead to the world of the living. The dreamers themselves are in a state where they are not quite dead, and the specters, though conscious, are not quite alive. As such, this creates a liminal boundary for both states, and the two approaches are both opposite and complementary.

The association between dreams and death could not be rendered any clearer. Both occur in an incorporeal state, in which the soul or eidolon is free. Because both of these involve similar states the *Atharva Veda* says that dreams originate from Yama's domain, the realm of the dead. It also explains the portrayal of Hypnos and Thanatos as siblings in the *Iliad*. The earlier cited depiction of the Great Lady (*Potnia Chthon*) who sends 'black winged dreams' also serves to strengthen the association between dreams and death, for Tartaros and Hades, were both originally likened to air and kingdoms of immaterial void and darkness. These descriptions refer to a subterranean *hypogeios* or 'below Ge', which describes a celestial hemisphere, curved beneath the earth.[49] Tartaros was a region of dense cold air without light, and Hades was often spoken of as having wings, just as in the *Epic of Gilgamesh*, where "Enkidu dreams of his death as a transformation into a bird, his

---

[49]   HILLMAN, J., *The Dream and the Underworld*, 39

arms covered with feathers; the dead are clad like birds, their element evidently air."[50] The relationship between birds and the dead is found in many cultures, and birds are often regarded as *psychopomps* or emissaries of the dead. Thus when the Great Lady is evoked, she is referred to as the mother of a domain beneath the ground, she gives flight to dreams from beneath the earth, just as the dead are buried within the earth, gestating until they awaken in the next world.

It is evident that there is a connection between the domain of dreams and the chthonic realm, since both concepts are related to the transmigration or projection of the soul/eidolon during death or sleep. This correspondence is, however, complicated by the fact that there seems to be some confusion in mythological records between what is chthonic (below ground) and what is, in fact, the earth itself (ground). The most logical explanation for this juxtaposition is that somehow myths relating to the Underworld become confused with that of the earth. Due to the earth's location above the chthonic world, it is an obvious metaphor for a gateway into the hidden depths. Because the process of dying and the state of sleep generate alterations in perception, it is more reasonable to associate dreams with the chthonic world than with the physical earth. The pairing of Hypnos and Thanatos likewise points to this association. It is also important to note that in the case of the deities associated with the

---

[50] HILLMAN, J., *The Dream and the Underworld*, 39

Underworld and dreams, they are often located within the earth, in caves. In instances where dream incubation is performed in a temple, the chthonic elements are still present because of the state of mind of the practitioner. By releasing the soul or eidolon, the practitioner enters into a state of voluntary 'death', which is the mysterious esoteric practice of 'dying whilst alive'. Dreams and death both trade with the same currency – the human soul and this is the common element that binds their powerful transformational processes together.

NECROMANCY

The death-change comes.
Death is another life. We bow our heads
At going out, we think, and enter straight
Another golden chamber of the king's,
Larger than this we leave, and lovelier.
And then in shadowy glimpses, disconnect,
The story, flower-like, closes thus its leaves.
– Philip James Bailey, *Festus*

Dreams come from the Underworld, and are linked to the domain of death. This curious relationship between dreams and death becomes more apparent when oneiromancy is compared with another school of divination – necromancy. Despite its sinister reputation, necromancy was a very widespread practice throughout the ancient world. It was not associated with evil or horror in most circumstances, but instead was a socially acceptable form of magic in which one obtained a prophecy from the dead. Only later, when death became an object of fear rather than a natural part of the life cycle, did necromancy begin to take on the terrifying image it has today. In the Hellenic Tradition, necromancy was a fairly common practice, and often had no 'evil' connotations at all.

The origin of necromancy in Greece is an interesting topic, with a variety of sources attesting to different etymological terms and phrases. Beginning with nekuia and *nektomanteia* (which can be thought of as 'necromancy proper'), necromancy starts to appear in texts from the third century BCE onwards. *Nekuomantis* (prophet of the dead) is first found in the Augustan Strabo, and Ps.·Lycophron used the variant form *nekromantis* circa 196 BCE, also in a context indicating a primary meaning 'dead-man prophet'.[51] *Nekuomanteion* (neut. sing.) begins to be cited in the fifth century BCE. *Nekuomanteia* (the feminine-singular abstract) is found first in the Latinized form *Necyomantia*, as the title of a mime by the first-century BCE Laberius, and Cicero uses the Greek neuter plural term *nekuomanteia* to mean 'rites of divination from the dead', attributing their practice to Appius Claudius.[52]

An important term related to nekuomanteia is *psuchagōgos* (evocator of souls), also found first in the fifth century BCE.[53] The alternative name *psuchomantis* (prophet of souls) is used in a context denoting one who divined the future through the wisdom of his own living soul.[54] Phrynichus Arabius (second century CE) informs us that the ancients applied the term psuchogōgos to those who charmed the souls of the dead with certain acts of sorcery (*goēteiais*) and Synesius (fourth to fifth century CE) describes being attacked by ghosts sent into his

---

[51]   OGDEN, D., *Greek and Roman Necromancy*, 96

[52]   Ibid., xxxi

[53]   Ibid., xx

[54]   Ibid., 96

dreams by *psuchopompoi* (ghost-sending) *goëtes*."[55] These forms of magic are related, and both are linked to the Underworld domain. The etymology of the term *goës* indicates that psuchogōgia originally constituted the heart of the concept: it is a derivative of *goos* (mourning song) and *goaō* (sing a song of mourning), both of which stand in contrast to the *thrēnos*, the mourning song of funerary professionals. The original Indo-European root was *gow-, which, as Burkert notes, was onomatopoeic for grief.[56] Both psuchogōgia and goës originate from this root term, with goës eventually evolving to become the school of the occult known in modernity as the *Goetia*. As Cosmas states, "*Goëteia* is the calling-upon of evil demons that hang around tombs [...] Goëteia got its name from the gooi and thrēnoi of those around tombs."[57]

The original role of the goës appears to have been as an officiator of funeral rites/mourning chants, and this role progressed into being one that not only mourned the dead but could also communicate with them. Burkert argues that the goës is the Greek equivalent of a shaman, a medicine man who can conjure the dead – but, like other forms of direct access to the divine, the role became suppressed as access was institutionalized by the oracles.[58]

---

[55] OGDEN, D., *Greek and Roman Necromancy*, 96

[56] Ibid., 110

[57] Ibid.

[58] STONEMAN, R., *The Ancient Oracles: Making the Gods Speak*, 21

Another practice related to this comes from the Greek *Sophoi*, known in scholastic literature as *iatromanteis* (from *iatros*, "healer", and mantis, "seer"), who were believed to be able to detach their soul from their body via an altered state of consciousness. Among the practitioners cited in this category, we find Abaris of Hyperborea, Aristeas of Proconnesus, Epimenides of Crete, Phormio of Sparta, Polyaratus of Thasos, Pythagoras, Empedocles of Akragas, Empedotimus of Syracuse, and Hermotimus of Clazomenai.[59]

For traditional necromancy, location was important, and as we saw with the tale of Odysseus and his descent, many of the locales selected did entail a descent into the underworld dominion of Hades. The name for a necromantic shrine was nekuomanteion (prophecy-place of the dead), *psuchomanteion* (prophecy-place of ghosts), or alternatively *psuchagōgion* (drawing-place of ghosts).

In terms of actual geographical sites, a number of places are mentioned. Sophocles refers to an oracle of the dead at Tyrrhenia,[60] and a nekyomanteion at Ephyra, Pausanias refers to a necromantic shrine in Phigaleia as "an impressive and snake haunted spot",[61] and an entrance to Hades via a cave at Heracleia is mentioned by Heraclides Ponticus, who composed

---

[59] MIHAJ, A., Soul's Aitherial Abode According to the Poteidaia Epitaph and the Presocratic Philosophers in *Numen* 57, 572

[60] STONEMAN, R., *The Ancient Oracles: Making the Gods Speak*, 70

[61] Ibid.

several books about oracles and apparitions of the dead.[62] The nekuomanteion at Acheron is directly mentioned by four authors: Herodotus and Pausanias (both of whom use the term nekuomanteion) an Odyssey scholiast who mentions a *limnē Nekuopompos* (Lake Sending the Dead), and Lucius Ampelius speaks of a "descent to the dead below for the purpose of taking up prophecies".[63]

The majority of these locations were in underground complexes, but there is another distinctive feature which is of significance. They all have a location next to lakes or pools. Both Avernus and Acheron are thought to have had included lakeside precincts and out of the well-known nekuomanteion sites, Tainaron is the only one not associated with a lake or pool.[64] The lakes themselves are also described as still and *aornos* (birdless) which indicates that they possessed unusual geographic features. Descriptions of the lakes refer to them as lifeless and eerie, which suggests they are incapable of sustaining life, and are probably volcanic lakes. The presence of a volcanic lake would also fit perfectly with the imagery of being a conduit to Hades.

The Heracleia and Tainaron nekuomanteia were located in caves modified by tools, whereas the Acheron and Avernus nekuomanteia were beside lakes, with their configurations being reflected in

---

[62] STONEMAN, R., T*he Ancient Oracles: Making the Gods Speak,* 70

[63] OGDEN, D., *Greek and Roman Necromancy,* 44

[64] Ibid., pp. 35-36

the derived usages: an air vent in a mine, and a system for draining water from underground and distributing it over infertile ground.[65] In addition to the famous 'birdless' lakes of Avernus and the Thesprotian Acherusia, there are also a number of others, including one in Tartessos (Spain).[66]

In relation to the air vents and the lack of birds, one explanation is the presence of volcanic gases, which also have an effect on consciousness, hence their use as a mechanism in rites requiring an altered state of mind. Daniel Ogden here cites a theory on the volcanic nature of Avernus:

> The locals used to tell another myth that birds that flew over the gulf fell into the water because they were destroyed by gases that came off it, as in *ploutōnia* (sanctuaries with mephitic emissions). And they took this place for a *ploutōnion*, and they believed that the Cimmerians lived there. Those who had sacrificed in advance and propitiated the underworld powers sailed into it. There were priests to guide one through the process, who managed the place under contract. There is a source there of drinkable water by the sea, but all kept back from this, considering it to be the water of the Styx. And the oracle is situated somewhere there. And they took the hot springs nearby, and the Acherusian Lake, to be evidence of Pyriphlegethon.[67]

---

[65]   OGDEN, D., *Greek and Roman Necromancy,* 18

[66]   Ibid., 26

[67]   OGDEN, D., *Witchcraft and Ghosts in the Greek and Roman*

The proximity of hot springs, undrinkable water, and gases which are toxic to birds all suggest high volcanic/geothermal activity in the area at the time – which is not unlikely due to Greece being prone to seismic activity. Additionally, it is not unusual for such locations to be regarded as sacred sites for divinatory purposes. Delphi, the most famous of all Greek oracle sites was originally said to draw its power from a chasm deep in the earth, and it has been speculated that the first Pythias may have inhaled a gas released deep from within the earth. Another example concerning gases at these locations is found at Hierapolis in Phrygia, which continues to produce gaseous vapors today. Acharaca was also rumored to contain a *charōnion* which killed the healthy (human or animal) but cured the sick who would incubate there, or alternatively the priests of the sanctuary (who were rendered immune to the harmful effects of the gas by initiation) would incubate on their behalf and derive cure-prophecies from Gods in their dreams.[68]

Naturally, the practice of nekuia developed and expanded into further occult practices, which fell into the hands of sorcerers and magicians. It is at this point that 'necromancy proper' is encountered. Now the dead are no longer merely summoned, they are bound and impelled to carry out actions on the goēs behalf.

Worlds: A Source Book, 162

[68] OGDEN, D., *Greek and Roman Necromancy*, 26

As with the oracles, location is important for necromancy, and the obvious choices were tombs and sites of death, as spirits were thought to linger near these locations. Visits to tombs in traditional accounts of necromancy usually involved the digging of a pit, libations (milk, honey, water, and oil), and offerings (grain and flowers), and blood (*haimakouria*), together with associated animal sacrifice and prayers.[69] Whilst animal sacrifice is considered barbaric by all civilized humans, in the ancient world people slew animals regularly for meat – supermarkets did not exist. If you wanted to eat meat, you had to kill it, and people thought nothing of such activities. Obviously, humanity has moved on and no longer tolerates animal sacrifices. However, when reading historical accounts, it is important to remember that hundreds of years ago people had a different mindset to that of modern man.

Following the offerings and libations, there is strong evidence that the practitioner went to sleep and dreamed or incubated on top of the tomb. For example, the Pythagorean Apollonius of Tyana's consultation of Achilles coincided with him spending the night on his barrow, and Philostratus implies that he slept there. Plutarch's tale of the Pythagoreans implies that Theanor also slept at Lysis' tomb to receive his prophecy, and Pythagoras himself wittily affirmed that the dead spoke to the living in dreams.[70] Some of the dead even invited consultation

---

[69] OGDEN, D., *Greek and Roman Necromancy*, 7
[70] Ibid., 11

– Ammias, priestess of a mystery cult at Thyateira in Asia Minor, had a funerary altar which stated: "If anyone wishes to learn the truth from me, let him put what he wants in a prayer at the altar and he will obtain it by means of a vision during the night or the day."[71] Another necromantic technique utilizing dreams is found in the Pitys spells which describe laying out a dead body on ass hide inscribed with magical figures, stating that a dead man will stand beside one in the night, which seems to indicate that he will appear to one in a dream.[72]

---

[71] OGDEN, D., *Greek and Roman Necromancy*, 6

[72] Ibid., 79

CURSE TABLETS & EVOCATIONS

The notion that poetry is a kind of magic and that the poet knows secrets and has powers not shared by other men is deeply rooted in the human race.

– Sir Cecil Maurice Bowra, *The Heritage of Symbolism*

More often or not, the dead were used as an intermediary between the world of mortals and that of Hades and Persephone, who were implored to act at the magicians bequest, and persuaded Hades to deliver justice on the target of the spell. The dead were thus conceived of as a catalyst in the causal chain of a magical event involving the person laying the curse, the underworld divinities, and the victim, which draws an analogy with the juridical system. Primarily, when human law failed them, those skilled in the occult arts sought retribution, not via the legal system, but through Hades in his supreme role as Judge of the Dead. Hades, Persephone, and Hermes are all mentioned in a binding spell from the *Attic Curse Tablets*, which is based on a structure similar to that of the legal process found in the court of Athens.

The normal formula is *katadô or katagraphô pros ton Hermen* or *pros tên Persephonen*, I bind or I write down someone "in the presence of", "before Hermes, Persephone". *Pros* with accusative is often attested in the judicial realm.

It means "register someone with someone else," transferring someone into another person's power. In the realm of magic, the victim of the spell is transferred to, handed over, devoted to the powers of the underworld gods, a morbid act indeed. The metaphorical action of binding or writing down is similar to, or I would even say, is in analogy to "I indict someone before the courts of Athens."[73]

It can, therefore, be assumed that the intended recipient of the spell is not the dead themselves, and instead *they convey the message* to the underworld divinities. In a similar fashion, Plato himself states that the *daimōnes* are the medium for the prophetic arts, incantation, divination, and sorcery. The divine will not mingle directly with the human, and it is only through the mediation of the spirit world that man can have any communication, whether waking or sleeping, with a God.[74] The daimōnes are also said by Plutarch to be instrumental in running the oracles, and the souls of the dead had adopted this role already in the *Derveni Papyrus* of the late fifth century BCE.[75] This reveals the missing link between the world of dreams and that of death: the concept of the soul or spirit.

---

[73]   RIEß, W., *Agency on Attic Curse Tablets* (Universität Hamburg), 2

[74]   STONEMAN, R., *The Ancient Oracles: Making the Gods Speak,* 104

[75]   Ibid., 68

In a revealing passage from the play Helen, Euripides states that "when people die, their mind does not live on, but it retains an immortal consciousness once it has merged with the immortal *aither*".[76] This passage echoes the doctrine of Anaxagoras (by whom Euripides was influenced) in which, mind (*nous*) "is the finest of all things and the purest".[77] Zeus was also said to inhabit the aither, as it is written here: "Zeus, most glorious, most great, lord of the dark clouds who dwells in the aither."[78] The aither is, therefore, the domain of Zeus that the immortal part of consciousness returns to, whilst the mortal aspect remains bound to the chthonic world, as Euripides expresses.

> Now let the dead be laid in earth, and each part return thither whence it came into the light of day, the breath into the aither of heaven, the body into the earth. For the body is not ours in fee; we are but lifelong tenants; and after that, Earth that nursed it must take it back again.[79]

This is also echoed in the following funerary inscription, The epitaph, originally in the cemetery of Ceramicus and now located in the British Museum reads,

---

[76] MIHAJ, A., Soul's Aitherial Abode According to the Poteidaia Epitaph and the Presocratic Philosophers in *Numen* 57, 559

[77] Ibid.

[78] Ibid., pp. 562-563

[79] Ibid., 559

Aither has taken their souls, and earth their bodies. They were undone around the gates of Poteidaia. Of their foes, some have their portion in the grave, others fled and made a wall their sure hope of life. This state and people of Erechtheus mourns its citizens who died in the front ranks, before Poteidaia, children of the Athenians. They cast their lives into the scales in exchange for valor, and their country's glory (Peek 1955:8–9).[80]

There are, therefore two resting places for the dead in the Greek afterlife – the air takes the soul, the earth the body. This reveals another esoteric concept – there are two types of the dead, those who are bound to the earth, and those who have merged their immortal consciousness with the aither. This theory explains many concepts, including an explanation for katabasis, and the movement of the soul during sleep. Empedocles, for example, believed in *metempsychosis* (reincarnation or transmigration of the soul) and claimed to have memory of other lives, which provided him with special powers including prophecy and the ability to bring forth souls from Hades. This, of course, leads to another issue – why does the soul need to be free from the body to acquire these preternatural abilities?

Ammonius develops the view that the daimōnes are really disembodied souls. Lamprias, the

---

[80] MIHAJ, A., Soul's Aitherial Abode According to the Poteidaia Epitaph and the Presocratic Philosophers in *Numen* 57, 556

narrator, asks why souls should need to be disembodied to perceive the future, and offers the answer that the body obscures the soul's vision (432c).[81]

The soul, therefore, is something which is conceived of as being purified by the death process and rendered more powerful once freed from the corporeal form. In this manifestation, reasoning and faculty of thought are perfected, permitting a state of almost 'pure mind', albeit it detached from physical consciousness. In the material state, the senses obfuscate the truth via layers of illusion, thus clouding our perception in a similar manner to the Hindu idea of *maya*. It is for this reason that the spirits are conceived of as powerful occult intermediaries between the world of the Gods and mortals – freedom from the flesh has endowed them with new abilities.

As for the type of spirits evoked in necromantic procedures, certain forms were considered easier and more suitable for the purpose, such as those who had died recently, especially if their death had been violent or premature, as stated by Lucan, Phar.,6. 712, who describes using a man, whose throat had been recently cut and was not yet used to death, as an involuntary assistant.[82] In general, those who were conceived of as belonging to the category

---

[81] STONEMAN, R., *The Ancient Oracles: Making the Gods Speak*, 177

[82] ALFAYÉ, S., *Sit Tibi Terra Gravis: Magical-Religious Practices Against Restless Dead In The Ancient World* (University of Oxford), 187

of the 'restless dead' were considered suitable for necromancy. This included the *ataphoi, atelestoi,* or *insepulti* (the deceased who had not received the appropriate funerary rites or burial), the *aōroi* (those who had a premature death), the *biaiothanatoi* (those who had suffered an unpleasant or violent death) and the malevolent undead, the *larvae* or *lemures*.[83]

The Hellenic Tradition also mentions oracles who are undead mortals, such as the decapitated heads of Orpheus and Trophonius. Both heads take on an oracular function after death, inspired by the Jewish Teraphim tradition in which human skulls are used as oracles.[84] The Teraphim were later replaced by spirits in Middle Eastern magical traditions reliant on necromantia. Diogenes Laertius believes that the skill of the Persian magi came from their ability to see ghosts. Along similar lines, Phlegon tells a story of a boy who was eaten by a ghost, except his head, which then began to spontaneously cite oracles.[85] The oracles of Orpheus and Trophonius are alike in function and description. Both are decapitated heads that divulge prophecies, and their sacred sites are located deep underground. Stoneman notes the comparison between the two here,

> Orpheus had been dismembered by Thracian women, and his head cast into the sea. The oracle

---

[83] ALFAYÉ, S., *Sit Tibi Terra Gravis: Magical-Religious Practices Against Restless Dead In The Ancient World*, 187

[84] Ibid.

[85] STONEMAN, R., *The Ancient Oracles: Making the Gods Speak*, 69

it came to occupy is also beautifully illustrated by a fifth-century Attic vase (Schmidt 1972). This shows a man having climbed down a rope into a pit like cave and communicating with Orpheus' head, which nestles in a further cranny of its own. The oracle of Trophonius was configured in a similar way: one climbed down into a pit (by ladder) and then slid into a further hole at its base in order to communicate with Trophonius, who was, like Orpheus, at once both dead and alive (see Pausanias 9.39).[86]

Pausanias also provides an account describing consultations with Trophonius that took place by night and began with the sacrifice of a ram in a pit, which is a common feature in necromantic rites.[87] This suggests that though the oracular 'talking heads' do not specifically involve nekuia, they do contain necromantic elements and the practice balances precariously on the boundary of the living and the dead, belonging to neither world.

Of all the magical acts required to contact the dead, the most frequent techniques involved intermediary procedures, often in the form of what can be loosely termed as 'curse tablets', such as the *Attic Curse Tablets* which were cited earlier. These were inscriptions that were written to be read by the dead, or by the Gods of the Underworld themselves.

---

[86]   OGDEN, D., *Witchcraft and Ghosts in the Greek and Roman Worlds: A Source Book*, 171

[87]   OGDEN, D., *Greek and Roman Necromancy*, 81

Pella leaded curse tablet

They were therefore deposited in graves, wells, or hidden in sanctuaries – places that functioned as entrances to Hades. Curse tablets that specifically required spirits to carry out magical acts of binding were often deposited in underground bodies of water.[88] In some cases, the practitioners placed the tablets into the right hand of the corpse, hoping that the corpse would pollute the tablet and thus the name inscribed on it, eventually dragging the victim down with it into Hades.[89]

Interestingly enough, the deity most often cited in curse tablets is not Hades himself, but rather Hermes Katochos (Hermes the Restrainer).[90] Considering the role that Hermes plays as a *psychopompos* it is not surprising that he, instead of Hades, is the deity who most often called upon to escort the victim down into the Underworld.

On these tablets, and also in verbal components, the method used is what Plato refers to as 'exerting

---

[88] OGDEN, D., *Greek and Roman Necromancy* (USA: Princeton University Press, 2001), 48

[89] RIEß, W., *Agency on Attic Curse Tablets*, 4

[90] Ibid.

influence' or *peithō* (persuasion). Not only are rhetoric and magic equated from *Gorgias* on, it is viewed as a special kind of magic, with the gifted speaker being a magician who is able to enchant his audience and compel them to do whatever he or she wants. Plato explicitly speaks of peithō in characterizing the activities of the goētes versus the Gods. In these examples, the magician compels the Gods to help him, and to serve his needs. This is in accord with other theories on the use of language being linked to magic,[91] due to the ability of the performer to evoke an emotional response at both the participant and observer level. In the case of the *Attic Curse Tablets*, there is even a direct analogy to the Attic judicial system, where speakers sought to convince and to persuade the judges of their version of incidents via peithō.[92] This means that the agent of the curse renders the accused person subject to the jurisdiction of Hades, in his capacity as Judge of the Dead. This act of registering the victim with Hades endowed the dead, in turn, with extraordinary functions, and placed the victim on trial before Hades.[93] This activity is expressed by using the verb *hypēretein*. Hypēretein is related to *hypēretēs*, which means executioner in Attic legal language.[94] It is therefore not the Gods themselves who are mentioned on the tablets, but the souls of the dead which take the target down into

---

[91] TAUNTON, G., *Fate and the Twilight of the Gods: The Norns and an Exegesis of Voluspá* (Australia: Manticore Press, 2018)

[92] RIEß, W., *Agency on Attic Curse Tablets*, 3

[93] Ibid., 5

[94] Ibid., 6

Hades, upon the order of the chthonic deities who are evoked via magical means.[95]

Another example of a necromantic curse tablet from the *Papyri Graecae Magicae* follows similar outlines, but is much less horrific than the example in the *Attic Curse Tablets*, and the magician just wants to win at the races. However, the intended effects still remain unpleasant. Compared with the content found in the *Attic Curse Tablets* a few technical differences arise. Firstly, some of the elements utilized have an obvious Middle Eastern origin, and secondly the spirit is bound not only by the Underworld powers, but also by a variety of others. Furthermore, Hekate is mentioned in this specific example, and is the main deity to whom this tablet is addressed.

PAPYRI GRAECAE MAGICAE D.T. 242 – CURSE TABLET

I invoke you, whoever you are, spirit of the dead, IONA, the God who established earth and heaven. I bind you by oath, NEICHAROPLEX, the god who holds the power of the places down beneath. I bind you by oath, … the God … of the spirits. I bind you by oath, great AROUROBAARZAGRAN, the God of Necessity. I bind you by oath, BLABLEISPHTHEIBAL, the firstborn God of Earth "on which to lie(?)" I bind you, LAILAM, the God of

---

winds and spirits. I bind you ... RAPOKMEPH (?) the God who presides over all penalties of every living creature. I bind you, lord ACHRAMACHAMAREI, the God of the heavenly firmaments. I bind you, SALBALACHAOBRE, the God of the Underworld who lords over every living creature. I bind you, ARCHPHESON(?) of the Underworld, the God who leads departed souls, holy Hermes, the heavenly AONKREIPH, the terrestrial.... I bind you by oath, IAO, the God appointed over the giving of soul to everyone, GEGEGEN. I bind you, SEMESEILAM, the God who illuminates and darkens the world. I bind you, THOBARRABAU, the God of rebirth. I bind you, the God who ... the whole wine-troughs ... I bind you, AOABAOTH, the God of this day in which I bind you. I bind you, ISOS, the God who has the power of this hour in which I bind you. I bind you, IAO IBOEA, the God who lords over the heavenly firmaments. I bind you, ITHUAO, the God of heaven. I bind you, NEGEMPSENOPUENIPE, the God who gives thinking to each person as a favor. I bind you, CHOOICHAREAMON, the God who fashioned every kind of human being. I bind you, ECHETAROPSIEU, the God who granted vision to all men as a favor. I bind you, THESTHENOTHRIL. CHEAUNXIN, who granted as a favor to men movement by the joints of the body. I bind you, PHNOUPHOBOEN, the Father-of-Father God. I bind you, NETHMOMAO, the God who has given you (the corpse) the gift of sleep and freed you from the chains of life. I bind you, NACHAR, the God who is the master of all tales. I bind you,

STHOMBLOEN, the God who is lord over slumber. I bind you, OE IAO EEEAPH, the God of the air, the sea, the subterranean world, and the heavens, the God who has produced the beginning of the seas, the only-begotten one who appeared out of himself, the one who holds the power of fire, of water, of the earth and of the air. I further bind you, AKTI ... PHI ERESCHEICHAL NEBOUTOSOUANT, throughout the earth (by?) names of triple-form Hekate, the tremor-bearing, scourge-bearing, torch-carrying, golden-slippered-blood-sucking-netherworldly and horse-riding (?) one. I utter to you the true name that shakes Tartarus, earth, the deeps and heaven, PHORBABORPHORBABORPHOROR BA SUNETEIRO MOLTIEAIO PROTECTOR NAPUPHERAIO NECESSITY MASKELLI MASKELLO PHNOUKENTABAOTH OREOBARZARGRA ESTHANCHOUCHENCHOUCHEOCH, in order that you serve me in the circus on the eighth of November and bind every limb, every sinew, the shoulders, the wrists, and the ankles of the charioteers of the Red Team: Olympos, Olympianos, Scorteus, and Iuvencus. Torture their thoughts, their minds, and their senses so that they do not know what they are doing. Pluck out their eyes so that they cannot see, neither they nor their horses which they are about to drive: the Egyptian steed Kallidromos and any other horse teamed with them; Valentinus and Lampadios ... Maurus who belongs to Lampadius; Chrysaspis, Juba and Indos, Palmatus and Superbus ... Boubalus who belong to Censorapus; and Ereina. If he should ride any other horse instead of them, or if some other horse is teamed with these, let them [not] outdistance [their foes] lest they ride to victory.[96]

In another spell to produce a ghostly assistant we also find Hekate mentioned. In the following example, Pitys relates instructions to King Ostanes, in which he teaches him the following necromantic rite.

Take an ass' skin, dry it in the shade, and draw on it the figure that will be revealed and the following text, in a circle:

AAMASI   NOUTHI   APHTHECHEMBÔCH POUPAIEICHNERI TA LOUTHIANI SERANOMÊGRENTI

EI BIL LONOUCHICH EITA PHOR CHORTOMNOUTHI THRACH PHIBÔBI ANTERÔ

POCHORTHAROCH EBOCH LESANOUACH PHEORÔBIS TRAION KÔBI IOUNIA

SAPHÔBI CHIMNOUTHI ASRÔ CHNOUPHNEN PHARMI BOLCHOSÊTH EPHOUKTERÔ

ABDIDANPITAAU EAE BOL SACHU ACHCHERIMA EMINTO RÔÔRIA EN AMOUN

AKREMPHTHO OUTRAUNIEL LABOCH PHERACHI AMENBOL BÊCH OS-TAOUA

---

[96]   GAGER, J., (trans.), *Papyri Graecae Magicae*, D.T. 242 –Curse Tablet, (1992), no. 10) - http://hermetic.com/pgm/dt-242.html

BELTHO

I conjure you, daimōn of a dead man [nekydaimōn] by the strong and implacable God and by his holy names, to stand yourself at my side in the coming night, in the form you used to have, and tell me whether you are able to perform the task. Now, now, quickly, quickly!

Then go swiftly to a place where there is a burial, or where something has been disposed of if you do not have a burial. Spread the hide underneath at sunset. Go back home and he will, by all means, come to you and stand himself by you on that night. He reports to you the manner of his death and first, he will tell you whether he has the strength to do anything or undertake any service for you.

Take a flax leaf and draw on it the Goddess who will be revealed to you with the ink which will be revealed to you, and write this spell in a circle (and place the leaf, spread out, on the head and garland it with black ivy, and by all means he will stand himself beside you during the night, in your dreams, and will ask you what you want, with the words, "Instruct me what you wish, and I do it"):

PHOUBEL TAUTHU ALDE MINÔOURITHI SENECHÔ CHELÊTHICHITIATH MOU

CHÔ ARIANTA NARACHI MASKELLI (VERBAL FORMULA) AEBITHÔ ACHAIL

CHAÔSOUNISOU SOUNIARTENÔPH ARCHEREPHTHOUMI BOLPHAI ARÔCHÔ ABMENTHÔ PHORPHORBA CHNOUCHIO-CHOIME

"I conjure you, daimōn of a dead man, by the Necessity of Necessities, to come to me, on today's day, on today's night and to consent to serve me. If not, expect other punishments." As soon as he agrees, get up at once, take a hieratic papyrus roll and draw on it with the black ink that will be revealed the figure that will be revealed, and write this spell in a circle and set it before him. He will immediately attract and he will do it without delay, not delaying a single day, even if you do not have any of the person's stuff [ousia] to control them with.

Often you will have no need of the flax leaf. In a second version of the spell, the papyrus itself will be laid down after you have ordered him to serve you. He attracts people, he lays them down on a sickbed, he sends dreams, he restrains and he procures revelations in dreams too. This spell alone can do all these things. Just modify the commonplaces in accordance with your project. Most of the mages, who carried their equipment with them, laid it aside and used him as an assistant.

They accomplished the things laid out here with all speed. For the technique is without all those needless extra words, but it completes the things laid out here quickly and with all ease.

Formula: "I say to you, daimôn under the earth, for whom the stuff [ousia] of this woman (or man) has been embodied on this night, travel to where she (or he) lives and bring her to me, either in the middle of the night or at any rate quickly. Accomplish the deed, because it is wished and commanded of you by the holy God Osiris KMÊPHI SRÔ."

"Accomplish, daimōn, the things written here. If you do accomplish them, I shall repay you with a sacrifice, but, if you are slow about it, may I inflict upon you punishments you cannot bear."

"Accomplish for me the deed, now, now, quickly, quickly." The black ink for the technique: The skin is inscribed with blood from the heart of a sacrificed ass, with which a bronzesmith's soot is mixed. The flax leaf is inscribed with hawk's blood, with which a goldsmith's soot is mixed. The hieratic papyrus roll is inscribed with eel's blood, with which *acacia* is mixed. Do these things as prescribed, and may you know, when you have completed them, what a powerful nature this technique encompasses, for in all convenience it treats the assistant as its equipment. Protect yourself with whatever form of phylactery you like.

Here is the figure drawn on the skin: A humanoid figure, with the head of a lion, wearing a belt, brandishing a staff in the right hand, on which there is to be a snake. An asp is to be wound around the whole of his left arm, and the lion's mouth is to breathe forth fire.

This is the figure on the flax leaf: Three-headed Hecate, with six hands, holding torches in her hands. The head on the right as you look at her is to be that of an ox, the head on the left that of a dog, the one in the middle that of a maiden. She is to have sandals on her feet.[97]

Finally, no examination of necromancy would be complete without a look at 'reanimation necromancy' – the act of physically resurrecting the dead and the zombie myth with which we are all now very familiar, thanks to a dearth of Hollywood films. Unlike other necromantic rites, this was not tied to geographic locations and could be performed anywhere – however, as would be expected, there are no historical accounts of reanimation necromancy, only fictional ones. In regards to the fictional accounts, we have three major surviving renditions: that of Lucan's *Erictho*, Heliodorus' old woman of *Bessa*, and Apuleius' account of *Zatchlas and Thelyphron*.[98] Of these depictions, the best is Lucan's *Erictho*:

---

[97] OGDEN, D., *Witchcraft and Ghosts in the Greek and Roman Worlds: A Source Book*, pp. 172-173
[98] Ibid., 163

"Furies; Crimes of the Styx; Punishments [Poenae] of the guilty; Chaos, you who long to confound unnumbered worlds; Hades, Ruler in the earth, for whom the death of gods, deferred across long ages, is agonizing; Styx; Elysium, the reward of no Thessalian woman; Persephone, you who detest heaven and your mother; Hekate, the lowest manifestation of my Goddess, by whose grace the ghosts and I hold converse, with silent tongue; Door-keeper of the broad house, you who throw human guts to the cruel dog; sister-Fates, destined to take up the threads of a life again and continue spinning; ferry-man of the flaming wave, reduced to a worn out old man by all the ghosts returning for me: hear my prayers. If I invoke you with a mouth sufficiently criminal and corrupt, if I never sing these incantations without first sating myself on human meat, if I have repeatedly opened up breasts, with the souls still in them, and rinsed them in warm brains, if any baby had been destined to live before it placed its head and entrails on your dishes, obey my prayer. I do not ask for a soul lying hidden in the cave of Tartarus and long accustomed to the dark, but one that is only just now abandoning the light and coming down. He still hesitates at the edge of the abyss of colorless Orcus, and, even if he does give heed to these spells [or: drink down these herbal potions], he will still only join the other ghosts once. Let this Pompeian ghost, until recently our soldier, prophesy everything to Pompey's son if you are properly honored by civil war."

This reanimation technique has much in common with the description of Medea's rejuvenation in Ovid's *Metamorphoses*, which raises the possibility that Ovid and Lucan are both referring to an earlier description of 'reanimation necromancy.'[99] The use of ingredients by Lucan is also of interest, as it is not entirely random or coincidental. Erictho's employment of moon-juice alludes to the drawing-down of the moon: it was supposed to deposit a foam on plants when brought low, which could then be collected up for magical purposes and other specialties such as the Arabian flying snake and phoenix described by Herodotus. However, this is all suggestive of further references to the extended influence of the Persian Magi being popularized in fiction, given that these accounts seem rather far-fetched. The strange and terrible noise with which Erictho begins her spell also seems to have been completely inarticulate, unlike the *voces magicae*.[100] This all suggests that Lucan's account was at best, very loosely based on facts, and should be regarded as an example of early Greek horror fiction rather than an actual account of necromantia. Lucan also revisits the topic in his work *Menippus* or *Nekuomanteia*, in which Menippus is taken down to the Underworld by a Chaldean necromancer to learn the secret of life from the ghost of Tiresias.[101]

---

[99] OGDEN, D., *Witchcraft and Ghosts in the Greek and Roman Worlds: A Source Book*, 167

[100] Ibid.

[101] OGDEN, D., *Greek and Roman Necromancy*, XXVIII

CONCLUSION

All men dream: but not equally. Those who dream by night in the dusty recesses of their minds wake in the day to find that it was vanity: but the dreamers of the day are dangerous men, for they may act their dream with open eyes, to make it possible. This I did.

– T. E. Lawrence

From the fluid world of dreams to the shadowed halls of the dead, one thing is clear: the border betwixt life and death is as thin as the gossamer of butterfly wings. A skilled practitioner in the Hellenic Mantic Tradition could project their soul outwards via the practices of katabasis and dream incubation or coerce the dead from Hades with the correct rites and offerings.

The proximity of both the Land of Dreams and the Land of the Dead is not coincidental – both are located deep underground, in the chthonic dominion of Hades and other otherworld deities such as Demeter, Persephone, Hecate and even the psychopomp Hermes. They are associated with serpents and gestation deep within the womb of the earth, in realms untouched by light where the rivers Acheron and Cocytus flow. All of this is symbolic of the twilight regions of the mind where subconsciousness thought emanates from. It is for this reason that the practices of oneiromancy and necromancy are linked, for both draw their power from the inner world of the subconscious and the corresponding chthonic powers. The practices are also linked together via the concept of the soul, which departs the body in both dreams and death. This raises an intriguing prospect for the interpretation of death and the dying process, for mythic sources present two options: there is an afterlife in which one remains bound to this world and one in which the soul returns to the aither. One is a uranic path to the light, the other is the chthonic path of shadows.

Of the two varieties of spirits, those used in necromancy clearly belong to the category of the troubled, earth-bound dead who are easier to evoke. It is these spirits who act as the intermediaries in necromancy, and all subsidiary forms of the occult later derived from it, including the goetia and European grimoires. In the *Attic Curse Tablets*, it is clear that the message is relayed to Hades, via the dead, and it is Hades that passes a juridical verdict on the victim. Other curse tablets and poppets were similarly placed in tombs, in the hope that the dead would take the victim down to Hades with them.

As for the fictional accounts of physically resurrecting the dead, these are exactly that—*fiction*—based on some popular magic techniques which were well known at the time and turned into the equivalent of an 'ancient zombie Hollywood film.'

Made in the USA
Monee, IL
30 June 2022